Praise for *Semper Parents*

" ... The pages contained in this book should be read by every American servicemember, their parents, and their grandparents. Today the services welcome family involvement like never before—and that is a good thing. Mary Regner informs that involvement by addressing virtually every aspect of service life, from boot camp through retirement, in short passages of wisdom drawn from her decades of experience supporting both her husband and their son in their Marine Corps careers. The title may make you think Marine, but my conviction is that the lessons on relationships, deployments, transfers, and even tragedy have broad application across all services; only the acronyms may differ. *Semper Parents* is an easy read, made even more so by Mary's relaxed and personal style of storytelling. Take this book home and you will enjoy it immensely!"

—General James Conway, (Ret),
34th Commandant, US Marine Corps

"What a blessing *Semper Parents* is! Mary's guide for parents of Marines, whether new recruits or seasoned warriors, is a critical 'mission brief' that pulls back the curtain on service in the Marine Corps and warmly welcomes parents into their new military family. *Semper Parents* is the perfect gift for Marine moms and dads, offering information, insights, and inspiration. The personal stories from Mary and other Marine parents will make you laugh, cry, well up with pride, and above all understand and appreciate the demanding and rewarding career your son or daughter has chosen. *Semper Parents* is a must read for all Marine parents!"

—Bonnie Carroll, president and founder,
Tragedy Assistance Program for Survivors

"For many decades, military spouses have shared their valuable knowledge and experience with other spouses to ease their time in service to this country. Mary Regner's book, *Semper Parents: Supporting Your Marine and Sharing the Journey*, presents this information to parents and other family members in a well-organized and easy to understand manner. This is the first time I've seen everything you need to know to support your Marine in one resource. *Semper Parents* should be on every Marine parent's reading list. You'll find yourself referring to it throughout the years, gaining strength from stories shared by people who've been there. Enjoy!"

—Mrs. Ellyn Dunford, 35-year Marine Corps spouse

"The guide all Marine parents need ... shows how parents can join their Marine on this incredible and sometimes terrifying journey. The nuggets of wisdom and personal anecdotes are something any military family can learn from. Read it, keep it nearby, and give it as a gift to the military family members you care about most."

—Besa Pinchotti, executive director and CEO
National Military Family Association

"... an invaluable guide to help navigate the trials, tribulations, and beautiful victories of those serving and the family members who endure the journey of service with them. I wish my family had this book when Kyle was injured in Afghanistan, but I am so thankful to Mary for the future generation of Marines and their families she will help with this book. *Semper Fidelis*, the Marine Corps motto, means always faithful and this book is a testament on how to be just that."

— Robin Carpenter, mother of
Medal of Honor recipient Corporal Kyle Carpenter

"When I was newly married to my Marine, I recognized Mary in the Camp Pendleton Commissary parking lot and chased her down, desperate for advice. ... she took me under her wing and became my military mom. ... she was the perfect example to a young newlywed of how to ... embrace this amazing journey. ... With her many years of experience as a military wife, military mom, in-law, and grandparent, there is no one better to help families navigate how to best support their military family member ... get this book and a highlighter for your family and tell them this is their official manual."

—Mollie Gross, comedienne and author of *Confessions of a Military Wife*

"Life is better with a mentor, and *Semper Parents* by Mary Regner is exactly that for *anyone* who has a loved one serving in the US Marine Corps—not just parents! ... Mary provides insight into everything from the mission of the Marine Corps, to family life, to career paths, to long-distance relationships ... *Semper Parents* is the best guide I have ever seen for any family member or friend who seeks a deeper understanding of Marine Corps life in order to provide greater support ... for their Marine."

—Michael McNamara, president, All Marine Radio

"... a compassionate, informative book that will be a guide and comfort to parents who find themselves part of a Blue Star Family. It is full of practical advice and wisdom to help understand and support the important the work of the Marines ... and their spouses and children."

—Kathy Roth-Douquet, cofounder and CEO, Blue Star Families

Semper Parents

*Supporting Your Marine
and Sharing the Journey*

Mary Regner

Elva Resa ∗ Saint Paul

Semper Parents: Supporting Your Marine and Sharing the Journey
©2022 Mary Regner
All rights reserved.

Library of Congress Control Number: 2022936500

ISBNs: 978-1-934617-64-9 (pb), 978-1-934617-69-4 (epub)

1L 2 3 4 5

Elva Resa Publishing
8362 Tamarack Vlg, Ste 119-106
St Paul, MN 55125

ElvaResa.com
MilitaryFamilyBooks.com

To the Blue Star and Gold Star families whose sons and daughters
swore an oath of loyalty, service, and sacrifice
to our great United States of America.

To my family, who shared our journey in the Marine Corps,
in the past, present, and future.

May God be with us all.
Semper Fidelis!
—Mary

Contents

Introduction	The Mission	1
Chapter One	New Relationships	7
Chapter Two	Next Adventures	21
Chapter Three	Semper Family	41
Chapter Four	Long-Distance Grandparents	53
Chapter Five	What If? What Next?	75
Chapter Six	Fears Realized	83
Chapter Seven	Turning Pride into Purpose	99
Chapter Eight	Careers and Transitions	105
Chapter Nine	Ceremonies and Celebrations	119
Closing	Staying Faithful	139
Appendix A	Marine Corps 101	141
Acknowledgments		165

The Mission

WELCOME TO THE MARINE CORPS! When your child joins the Marine Corps, you become part of the Marine Corps extended family. Since 1775, the Marine Corps has maintained rich traditions and a strong, supportive community. And you are now part of that history and community. This new step in your life will naturally be filled with many questions, concerns, hopes, and expectations. For some, service to country is a family tradition. For others, it's a brand-new adventure. Your mission is to support this choice your Marine has made and to sustain a meaningful relationship throughout their service.

I had many mixed feelings when our son unexpectedly announced his desire to become a Marine. At the time, my husband had been serving in the Marine Corps for more than twenty years, but being the parent of a Marine felt quite different. Having our son serve as a Marine elicited many different emotions. Our pride was mixed with a dose of reality. My husband was proud and excited to hear this news and felt confident that the leadership qualities our son exhibited in scouting and athletics would help him succeed. From a spouse's perspective, experiencing my husband's many years of military training, deployments, and combat assignments made me aware of the risks as well as the rewards. What that might look like for our son, and how I would handle those situations as his mom, remained unclear.

Knowing our son's decision was his to make, our honor from that moment was to support him as best we knew how. And now we have been Marine parents for more than two decades. We supported our son through three combat tours, multiple deployments, and many moves. We welcomed his bride into our family, and the grandchildren that followed. Our roles and levels of support changed as the years flew by, but our commitment remains unwavering. As seasoned Marine parents, we hope our experiences, and the resources we have come to know and rely on, will be of value and use to you in the months and years to come, especially if military service is a new experience for your family.

This guide is designed to educate, enlighten, encourage, and motivate you as a key stakeholder in the safety, security, and success of your Marine. However, this is not a "How to Be a Marine" manual. The Corps and its very capable leaders at all ranks are well equipped to inform and mentor Marines. My goal is to provide information and perspective to help you as a parent have confidence in your unique ability to best support your Marine.

The first moment you realized your child wanted to become a Marine may have been life changing. Mine was. The emotional roller coaster included highs and lows of excitement and worry, clear information and confusion, joy and grief. All those feelings are normal. Perhaps you have had times when you engaged in tough conversations with your Marine or with the recruiters. Maybe you shed a few tears on the day your child shipped out to Boot Camp or Officer Candidate School (OCS) or The Basic School (TBS). But you each made it through to their graduation. Now is a good time to explore those growth moments. Or perhaps your Marine will soon depart for the start of their training. You will likely notice how your new Marine is changing.

Though I am the parent of a Marine, this is not a story about how my husband and I raised our son to be a Marine, nor is this about his career. We share stories, thoughts, tips, and reactions from many other parents and from our own experiences to help you and other parents navigate the Marine parent journey, filled with vulnerable, scary moments as well as celebrations.

Each young Marine has a unique experience entering the Corps. Since the Marines were first formed in 1775, our country has asked its citizens to fight and defend US freedom and protect our way of life. History has demonstrated that our country will call on Marines time and again for their service.

Our country drafted its young people into military service in World War II on two front lines across the Pacific and Atlantic, and again in Korea and Vietnam. When the United States abolished the draft and converted to an all-volunteer force in 1973, those who continued to serve faced conflicts in Beirut and Operation Desert Storm. Our military required new resolve to defend our country following terrorist attacks on September 11, 2001, in New York City, at the Pentagon, and in the skies over Shanksville, Pennsylvania. Your Marine volunteered for the opportunity to serve the uncertain demands of tomorrow.

The ways families stay connected and the requirements, skills, and abilities needed on the battlefield change over time. Organizational structures, strategies, and equipment have changed considerably since November 10, 1775, but the allegiance service members pledge—to protect and defend the constitution and our democracy—has not changed. Whether you served or had family members serving in the Marine Corps ten, twenty, or thirty years ago, the same core values of honor, courage, and commitment remain, even as new advancements in warfare, job descriptions, technology, and mission requirements have evolved to meet the needs of the battlefield and the Corps.

Marine Corps history is filled with stories that show flexibility and adaptability, along with creativity, bravery, and heroism. Each new member brings their own background of skills, knowledge, culture, and many other characteristics that form their personality, values, and attitude. These characteristics and behaviors were inherited from the beginning and influenced by you, their family.

This book provides Marine parents information about the life cycle of a Marine from recruitment through transition beyond the uniform. This journey has many points on the road, highlighted by training, ceremonies, deployments, special duty assignments, more deployments, schools, milestone events, and more deployments. No two Marines follow the same path. Each has different skills, duty stations, uniforms, medals, and awards, but all Marines share a standard of excellence. They become a larger family as they walk their career path together.

Parents, guardians, grandparents, teachers, coaches, friends, and others who raised, supported, disciplined, or guided your Marine throughout their young life, influenced their behaviors, goals, and outcomes, making each person a part of your Marine's "hometown" family. You will have the privilege of sharing love, joys, and sorrows of the life this Marine has just entered.

I interviewed many families for this book. Some say their child was born to join the Corps, and others describe the decision as a complete surprise. Whatever led to the decision, at the point it became a reality, the parents' resolve to be supportive has had a positive and lasting impact on their relationship with their Marine.

As the chapters unfold, the topics build on new knowledge and experiences, from recruitment through transition or retirement. Each message speaks from a different perspective—the Marine's, the spouse's, or parent's—regarding milestones in life, marriage and children, as well as promotions, deployments, duty stations, and special assignments. Stories of achievements and successes are mixed with the realities of injury, divorce, trauma, and death. In addition to a snapshot of policies, conditions, resources, and opinions of our time, this book offers scenarios, realities, and resources to help you better understand how to support and survive the challenges, tragedies, and celebrations of being a Marine parent.

People who shared their stories and best practices with me—from top leadership of the Corps to new Marines, parents of new recruits to Gold Star parents, caregivers, relief agencies, and nonprofit groups—did so with a desire to help new Marine parents gain a broad view of life in the Corps.

Their input is only one aspect of this book. You will complete the "rest of the story" as your Marine's journey unfolds. Honor, courage, and commitment are the values your Marine holds dear. I hope you will build on the legacy of service, adventure, duty, and sacrifice, and share their journey!

This project has been a voyage of discovery. The topics presented developed as I engaged with various stakeholders and experts. The categories of support I include in the book are a sampling of lifestyle needs of the Marine from recruitment through transition: training, career development, deployments, moves, special assignments, growing into adulthood, and supporting their own families.

If you have questions or concerns (*What does this mean? Is this normal? Will my Marine be okay? Will I be able to deal with things I have no control over?*), I hope this book will make answering these questions easier, and help enhance and sustain the relationship between you and your Marine throughout your Marine's career.

While your Marine will have support from dedicated leaders and advocates inside the Corps, you will be an integral part of your Marine's personal support team. I hope the stories, tips, and life experiences shared in this book help you find ways to nurture that relationship.

Let the journey begin!

Chapter One

New Relationships

PARENTS ARE OFTEN THE FIRST and most important relationship a child develops throughout their life. That relationship evolves as a child matures from infant to toddler, tween to teen, and into an adult. For the Marine parent, the relationship shifts from parent of their young adult, to parent of their Marine. Many parents shared with me how they forged a new role in the life of their Marine. Your relationship with your child is unique. Some changes are natural regardless of career choice as your child grows more independent. Marine Corps life will also demand adjustments from both of you, and a supportive relationship can ease the way.

Whether you have prior experience with military life or not, have other children who have already grown into adults, or this adventure is all new, you will likely feel a range of emotions as you accept your child's career choice and discern the dynamics of your relationship going forward.

Bonnie, a Marine mom, shares:

> My son is about to be a third generation Marine. He has always wanted to be a Marine. Always. Although he was adamant about not wanting to go to college, his father and I insisted he take the SAT and apply to multiple colleges during his senior year of high school. We wanted him to have choices. We wanted him to change his mind. College acceptance

letters flowed in and he could have attended any number of schools, but he wanted to be a Marine. So in just over a month, my son will begin his quest to be a Marine.

The world is not a safe place. It is not any safer now than it was ten years ago when my husband donned combat gear and fought alongside his band of brothers. My husband has shared the realities of war with my son, yet he is undeterred. I can see the thought ticking across his forehead like a banner on the evening news.

Sending off a son and daughter—yes, my daughter also plans on joining the family business and aspires to be a Marine later this summer—is not for the faint of heart. Yes, I admit to a swell of pride as folks acknowledge their willingness to serve, but my heart skips a beat when I read about service members struggling with injuries, especially the unseen signature PTSD injury. We have come a long way in identifying PTSD and offering treatments and interventions that ease the symptoms and quiet the storm for many of our service members.

I am an institutional girl, born and raised in the Army, then married a Marine. I was the quintessential active-duty spouse: the family readiness volunteer who brings cookies, a friendly face on move-in-day type. I get the lifestyle. Love the lifestyle, as a wife. As a mom, well, that's different.

What am I supposed to do with my mother-bear instincts? The primal need to protect? Will my son's commander let me follow him into the field? Can I fight off the terrorists before they get to him, much less our country? He is my son. I am his mother. It is not particularly difficult for me to admit to having mixed feelings about the service of my children.

Many things in life present a paradox. My son and daughter will not be deterred from service. They are called to serve. They can no more ignore the call than they can choose not to breathe.

But still the paradox exists, causing me to question, what is a mother to do? I am called to believe I can maintain a safe harbor at home. I can be the soft place for him to fall when he needs it. I can watch with pride as he realizes his dream of becoming a Marine, and I can be part of the cadre of moms who support the needs of our troops both deployed and at home.

Complex feelings and questions about becoming a Marine parent are normal. Military life comes with a fair amount of pride and joy, but also some uncertainty and worry. Your relationship with your Marine will continue to change and grow—at home, during deployments, throughout military traditions, and other life events during and after their time in service.

Knowing what to expect from the first few days, months, and years as a Marine parent will help you navigate and prepare for the transitions and relationships ahead. With each new phase of military life, you will have opportunities to connect with your Marine and experience the strong bond of the Marine Corps community.

Joining the Marine Corps is a choice and a journey that will impact your Marine for a lifetime. No matter how the commitment initiates—enlisting with a Marine Corps recruiter, participating in a Reserve Officers' Training Corps (ROTC) program at a college or university, or joining through an Officer Selection Officer—each new Marine signs a binding contract to dedicate a specific amount of time to the Corps. The initial total obligation is usually eight years, with an agreed-upon minimum active-duty requirement and the remaining years continuing on active duty or serving as a Reservist or Individual Ready Reservist (IRR) available to be called to active duty if needed.

Each enlisted recruit or officer candidate must undergo a series of physical and mental training challenges to prepare them for military life.

Boot Camp/Basic Training

Enlisted Marines attend a thirteen-week Marine Corps basic recruit training, or boot camp, at a Marine Corps Recruit Depot in either Parris Island, South Carolina, or San Diego, California. Officer basic training has two components. To become a commissioned officer, a candidate must first successfully complete Officer Candidate School (OCS), a 10-week program for college seniors and graduates in Quantico, Virginia. An enlisted Marine who wants to become an officer but does not have a college degree may participate in the Marine Enlisted Commissioning Education Program (MECEP). All newly-commissioned and appointed (warrant officer) Marine Corps officers attend The Basic School (TBS), a six-month training program at Quantico. Upon graduation from their respective basic training (boot camp or TBS), Marines are assigned their Military Occupational Specialty (MOS) and receive their initial assignments.

While this initial training looks slightly different between specific programs, the role of a Marine parent remains the same: to provide support from afar and let your Marine fully immerse themselves in this intense, exhausting initial training.

Marines typically cannot have direct contact with family during training. A significant portion of training is dedicated to testing their willpower and strength—something they can only do with fellow recruits or candidates. However, in the event of a family emergency, protocols are in place to deliver messages to your Marine.

Physical Training and Academics

The first few weeks of training involve instructions on military history, customs and courtesies, basic first aid, uniforms, leadership, and core values. Trainees begin to learn discipline through close-order drill (formal movements and formations used in marching, parades, and ceremonies) and hand-to-hand combat skills through the Marine Corps Martial Arts Program.

Survival is a word packed with thoughts of endurance, persistence, and beating the odds. As you imagine the challenges of basic training, what new activities can you challenge yourself to accomplish? Use this time for your own personal growth too. Do you want to get serious about exercising, eating well, or managing your stress? Such activities may be a key to your own survival as a Marine parent. During my son's basic training, I found that challenging myself to endure physical activities such as hiking, while he was facing endurance challenges, made me feel closer to him.

Before Boot Camp or OCS begins, you may want to set up a routine you will follow. Letter writing is an important priority. I often recommend new Marine parents connect to an online communication tool, such as Sandboxx.us, that enables your trainee to receive your letter within twenty-four hours of you sending it. Consider offering to write to other recruits or candidates who may not be receiving letters from home, to send encouragement their way. The bonds one makes in basic training can last a lifetime in the military. Your support will always be remembered.

This can be a good time to start researching and planning for graduation too. Dates are posted ahead of time. Look into options for where to stay and eat, as well as the graduation activities you won't want to miss. If you have to ask for vacation time from your employer, plan ahead to save yourself the stress later.

In the early weeks, you may find it useful to join an online group for support, information, and updates. Online sites may be monitored by officials of the training depots or administered by family members. Find a group that meets your needs. While the advice of other members may be helpful, rely on the Marine Corps training websites for official or special updates.

Team Building

Sometimes there is a break in the intense training to focus on community-oriented tasks, such as doing laundry, helping in the supply warehouse, and cleaning up the base before completing the final phase of training.

By that point, about a month of training is complete. That means you've been training to be a Marine parent for a month too. You may want to start exploring local patriotic community organizations. A Marine Corps League or an American Legion may host public activities and events that display their patriotism and respect for those who serve or have served. Each organization has specific membership requirements. Ask about that now so you will understand your eligibility to join organizations that interest you.

Marksmanship and Combat Training

Recruits and candidates learn Marine Corps Marksmanship and become familiar with weapons. Combat marksmanship, land navigation, and maneuvering under enemy fire are common training exercises.

Have you committed yourself to learning any new skills while your recruit is away? My good friend started playing pickleball and signed up for an online class through a local nature center while her recruit was in basic training.

Many parents are already working hard at their day jobs and possibly juggling other children's busy schedules or rebalancing responsibilities and family dynamics.

At home, if you are experiencing personal difficulties at this time, it can be a hard choice whether or not you should share this information during training. The same is true for information about friends or local news stories. Remember, trainees do not get cellphones, computers, or media reports while in training. In special circumstances, the Marine Corps may allow Boot Camp recruits to have access to their cellphones on a limited basis once they complete "the Crucible" phase of training.

Regarding situations at home, ask yourself if the issue or crisis could resolve itself in a short time or by reaching out to someone else who can help. If you do share the information, is it something your child can solve while in basic training? Consider how they will take the news. Will it distract them from focusing on their training? Drill instructors advise parents to only share difficult information in a letter after it has been fully resolved.

News of serious illness, injury, or death of an immediate family member should be reported through the Red Cross military help line, which will properly notify Marine Corps officials. They in turn will make the news known to the recruit and offer proper support.

Testing and Administrative Tasks

Boot Camp recruits undergo various academic and physical exams. They face a final fifty-four-hour field event known as "the Crucible," which tests them on the knowledge, skills, and values they were taught throughout training. Those who complete the final challenge are awarded their eagle, globe, and anchor, symbolizing their transformation from recruits to Marines.

Hopefully, you have been writing letters of encouragement during this especially challenging time. Your pep talks go a long way to getting your recruit through the final phase and most difficult period of training.

When you get the news that your Marine has received their eagle, globe, and anchor, start packing your bags and prepare to attend graduation. You are almost there!

Graduation is a time to celebrate what your Marine—and you—have accomplished during the training period. Enjoy! If for some reason you are unable to attend graduation, let your Marine know. Traditionally, the organization Stand Alone Marines (SAMs) offers volunteers who "stand in" for parents at graduation and following the ceremonies. The organization hosts a picnic for Marines whose families are unable to attend. No Marine stands alone!

By graduation time, you should know what kind of time off your Marine may have. Whether there is time between graduation and the start of a new Marine Corps assignment is up to the Marine Corps. Your Marine may be headed to a new location the day after graduation, or they might have a week off. If your Marine is able to return home before the next training begins, discuss those terms with your Marine to make their time well spent. They will be given travel orders to instruct them on their next check-in date, time, and place.

Life in the Corps

During training, parents and families can see week-by-week information about the activities their recruits and candidates were involved in. After this phase, public information about where your Marine is stationed, and what they are doing, is not always available. From this point on, each unit has their own website for general information. All official information is delivered through the Family Readiness Program official and a closed social media group in each individual command. Your Marine is the person who authorizes you to receive information from their unit. Remember, they may not be available to answer your calls or emails, so being connected through the family readiness representative is another option.

The Family Readiness Program keeps families informed through official communication about command news, troop movement, deployments, and other activities. Your Marine should be able to identify an official "go-to person" for their unit, in the early days of joining that new unit. Your Marine is able to include you on the list of family members allowed to receive news and information, or to be added to the official unit social media group.

The family readiness official, commander, Marines, and families work together to solve a variety of issues. Through resources or referrals, they connect Marines and their families to those who can help. In the case of a training accident or serious situation affecting the Marine or their family—for example, in the event of a local disaster—the command decides and coordinates when and how information is delivered.

While your child transformed into a Marine, you were learning how to be a Marine parent. As time goes on, your relationship may shift again. You each let go a little as the way you relate to each other changes from parent-and-child, to adult-and-adult. You may have moments when you temporarily lose your way in this transition, and that's normal. Keep up your spirits!

Communication

As a parent, you have likely offered advice to your Marine for many years on various topics. If you have not been on the best of terms, this separation makes communicating more challenging. Good and open communication is your best tool in this new relationship, regardless of your past. Honest discussions about what you can do to support your Marine have their place for loving and practical reasons. A topic of conversation about world affairs may enter into your conversations now, since there is a chance your Marine may become a part of the story firsthand. You may have critical opinions about our country's involvement, the Corps' leadership, or about elected officials. When you voice an opinion or have a question or concern about issues related to your Marine's mission or work, remember that your Marine is operating under a new set of ethics, strict rules, and laws that drive their responses, judgment, and decisions. Having a clear understanding of their rules, especially operational security (OPSEC), is critical to their safety. You have the right to express your opinion, but your Marine may avoid such discussions, or they may voice a different opinion as a sign of allegiance and respect to their command. They can still value and appreciate your support and unconditional love without engaging in conversations about politics or the Corps.

Your insights into your Marine's personality, mood, and motivations give you an advantage when encouraging your Marine. Parents and close family members can sense subtle emotional cues that mark their Marine's personality. You know what makes this person tick! Paying attention to these cues can help tremendously. You will know when you need to draw closer, through phone calls, texts, letters, or packages that show your support and encouragement. The stress of military service can expose young warriors to situations that test their resolve. Sometimes, hearing your voice or reading your letters will be just what they need.

Behavior

"Who are you, and what have you done with my kid?" one Marine mom asked when her son came home after boot camp. His behavior had changed in little ways, such as holding doors open for her and helping around the house. You might find your Marine has changed too, with a newfound level of concern for safety, rules, and proper behavior. Every Marine brings values with them to the Corps, from their upbringing and prior life experiences. The Corps shapes those values further with discipline and strength of mind. Many rules govern a Marine's behavior. For example, if a Marine is found using or being involved with others in possession of narcotics, or excessive or underage alcohol consumption, they may receive legal punishment or discharge, which may also jeopardize their security clearance status or future benefits.

When you are invited to attend graduation ceremonies or places where your Marine is stationed, your conduct demonstrates your respect for their job. Showing interest in your Marine's work is always in good taste. Following the guidelines for respect for the American flag and the national anthem also go a long way.

Eventually you will settle into a reasonable rhythm in your new relationship. Marines call it their "battle rhythm." You will notice a few terms and jargon that now pepper your Marine's conversation. Then a day will come when they make a reference to someone as their brother or sister, or their Marine mom. *Who are these people?* They are the ones supporting your child in their new military community. It could be the family of a Marine who lives near the base who opens their home on weekends. After spending a few weekends or sharing a holiday dinner with them, your Marine may consider them their California or North Carolina family. This is a good thing—an indication that new relationships are filling the void of the family life they miss. And these relationships can last a lifetime. Sometime in the future, you may become that

Marine mom or dad to a Marine you welcome into your home, and fill the void of a family who lives far away. That is a good thing too! It's how the Marine family works.

We hosted our son's friends a few times while he was at Officer Candidate School. What they appreciated was a home-cooked meal, a washing machine and dryer, and a quiet afternoon to relax or sleep. We also suggested they call home if they wanted to. Those were the best memories as a parent, when we could sit back and enjoy the moment. Soon enough, many miles would separate us, and those opportunities would be gone.

You may have concerns about your Marine being so far from home and feeling alone. The Corps supports programs to help Marines build healthy relationships within the Corps and in the local communities. The Single Marine Program (SMP) was designed to respond to the need for social activities and a community of support for single Marines and for married Marines stationed without their spouse or children. They promote leadership, service, fellowship, and new experiences.

I have observed the fun activities and club-like facilities that make this program so appealing, for instance, hiking, surfing, and kayaking adventures; special competitions; and reduced-price or free entertainment tickets to musical or sporting events. Being part of the Single Marine Program allows a Marine a voice on issues that affect the quality of everyday life in the Corps.

If your Marine wants to make a difference and represent the Corps in their local community, they will enjoy being involved with the Single Marine Program. Single Marines contribute tens of thousands of community service hours each year. SMP gives them the opportunity to volunteer for Habitat for Humanity, Toys for Tots, beach cleanups, or visits to veterans homes.

Taking on additional responsibilities while single builds confidence and creates an understanding of how to balance duty and off-duty time. Using free time to build relationships in healthy, safe environments with those who share similar values is the start of mature, lasting relationships.

Reading

I belong to a book club. I joined so I could open my eyes to people and places, cultures and new experiences different from my own. Sometimes I read for information, sometimes for pleasure, but each book exposes me to new thoughts and ideas, regardless of the topic. Your Marine is expected to read a variety of books for the same reason, but mainly for their professional development.

As you share new experiences with your Marine and the Marine Corps, you may want to seek reading materials related to the Marine Corps, world affairs, and travel.

The Commandant's Professional Reading List presents books most pertinent for professional development and critical thinking at each level of a Marine's career. These books serve to educate, inform, and inspire the reader about the history of the United States and the world; warfare strategies and philosophies; and stories of leadership, courage, and heroism. Requirements are listed for each specific rank. These are excellent books to give and receive, and they create opportunities for family members to find common ground when discussing topics that matter to your Marine. From these books, Marines learn leadership traits and principles of the Corps to develop their own leadership abilities and those of their subordinates. These topics have helped keep me informed and aware of affairs of the world where my Marine could be sent.

For advice on stress management, or other positive coping mechanisms, I recommend self-help books too. These books have been invaluable to me at times I knew the best thing I could do for my Marine was to learn more about taking care of myself.

Your Own Checklists

For their initial training and throughout their Marine Corps career, your Marine will use plenty of checklists. It may help you to begin creating your own lists and tips as well to ease your transition, maintain communication, and nurture your relationship. Some items on your list may be useful during training while others you will use later during a move or a deployment. One mom shared her thoughts to get you started, based on a packet she received from her son's recruiter before boot camp.

Well-being

- Start your day with gratitude. Keep a positive attitude, positive thoughts, and prayers for your Marine and yourself.
- Pack a small family picture and a send-off letter in your Marine's backpack on the day they ship out. It is like an extra hug goodbye.

Letters

- Write letters daily and number them. Include local and daily newsy items, as well as friend and family updates.
- If your Marine sends a discouraging letter, remain positive and encouraging. Their letters will change to "I can, and I will finish this" letters as their skill and confidence increases.
- Send pre-addressed envelopes and stamps for easy return mail.
- Ask family and friends to write to your Marine and send extra goodies in care packages to share.

Connections

- Ask your Marine to include you on the family readiness roster to receive official information.
- Join their unit's social media group.
- Read books to become more informed about the Corps, other families' experiences, or self-help resources. Join or start a book club with people who share mutual interests.
- Find a local military family, veterans group, or online community to share mutual support. Marine Corps League and Blue Star Families are a great start.

Memories

- Capture in pictures and words the moments before your Marine leaves home, during training if possible (check for Marine Corps online photos), and the celebrations.

- Keep a journal of your thoughts, so you can reflect later on ways you and your family are changing and growing.

- Create a photo book as a keepsake of this unique time in your life and theirs.

- Save their letters and look back on their growth and transition. They can do it and you can too!

⟶ Chapter Two ⟶

Next Adventures

A MARINE'S FIRST FEW ASSIGNMENTS after basic training may take them around the country or around the world. Some Marines are instructed to enter specialized training at a particular military base or to report to their first duty station. Others may receive orders to report to combat zones or natural disaster sites. The size of the unit could be as small as a Special Purpose Marine Air Ground Task Force (SPMAGTF), or as large as a Marine Expeditionary Force (MEF). Other missions are conducted by Marine Special Operations Command (MARSOC).

Your Marine may spend their first assignment local to their home base, with occasional temporary assignments or trainings nearby. They may know ahead of time that they will receive orders to deploy, such as being assigned to a Marine Expeditionary Unit (MEU) that will deploy with Navy ships on a set rotation. Or their unit may deploy unexpectedly.

For regular assignments, your Marine will receive Permanent Change of Station (PCS) orders stating the military base location and expected date the assignment begins. They may receive personal leave (vacation) days coinciding with their move. Details of some assignments are kept secret to keep troop movements and missions safe. Parents and families receive information, tips, and updates from the command through a Family Readiness Program representative, social media sites, and newsletters. This process is quite routine, even if the nature of an assignment or deployment is not. Letters, emails, and care packages may be the best ways to reach your Marine, even if they live nearby. Routine training can take up nearly their entire day, every day, while on assignment.

Once our Marine was assigned to a base for his first duty assignment, his life and ours settled into a normal routine. We were used to getting occasional phone calls to catch up on news. Pretty soon it was normal to not be concerned if we didn't hear from him. We all settled into this new normal. Daily prayers continued for his safety and the safety of his fellow Marines. Any change in the routine was met with updates and information as it was available. The cycles of deployments became more predictable, which helped brace me for unscheduled assignments or unexpected circumstances as our journey continued.

Deployments

The term deployment is used to distinguish when an individual or unit is sent away from their normal duty station to another location to accomplish a mission. Deployments may include short routine training assignments, lengthy combat missions, or humanitarian assistance. The location of a deployment is not always public, and time off to spend with family is not guaranteed.

When my Marine deployed for the first time, I had lots of questions. *How often should I write? How many packages should I send? When will I get to see my Marine again? How do we talk about or manage the departure and reunion occasions? How will I react if I am not able to attend the send offs or reunions?* I suggest writing a thoughtful letter of love and encouragement to your Marine prior to their leaving or a warm welcome home prior to their return. I wanted to know what worked best for my son, but I was not sure how to ask. With experience, I learned that these questions are best answered well in advance, because the period of time prior to deployment is packed with special training and exercises that make free time a rare commodity for a Marine.

Preparing your mindset to handle a deployment is critically

important. Your Marine will carry with them the tone you set for your relationship, so make it positive. Learning that your Marine will be deploying can cause anxiety and worry to creep into your conversations and interactions, so be mindful of the emotions and behaviors you experience surrounding the time of deployment. Keep in mind that your Marine is well trained and well led. Rather than dwell on factors you have no control over, focus on what you can control—how you behave and cope in order to maintain a healthy emotional attitude and mental wellness.

You can expect your Marine to have great stories to share from their experiences, even though you may not always be in steady communication. There are many reasons you may not hear from your Marine regularly during deployment, including poor or no internet connection, troop movements, or a need for caution with communication due to operational security (OPSEC). Enjoy any time you are able to see or hear them in live time, and explore new ways to connect while they are out of sight and out of touch.

Deployments can occur with notice or without much notice at all. Most active-duty Marines deploy with their local unit, and in that case, family support is coordinated around the families in that location with extended communications for parents. If a Marine is called to deploy from a Reserve status, support networks may be more challenging for families scattered in numerous hometown communities. If a Marine is an individual augmentee with orders to join a unit independently, they will be detached from their home unit for a period of time.

The duration of a deployment can be anywhere from two weeks to more than a year. The time between deployments, called dwell time, is used to train, repair, regroup, and restore a unit for deploying again. Since dwell times vary, your Marine's time away may be irregular and, due to OPSEC, difficult to explain.

Emotional Cycle of Deployment

Department of Defense (DoD) researchers have studied and documented emotions that Marines and their families experience during deployment. The Emotional Cycle of Deployment explains common feelings experienced before, during, and after deployments. Brought on by change, anxiety, or stress, these feelings are normal. Learning what your Marine may be experiencing, and recognizing your own emotions and how to manage them, makes the process easier to navigate and builds resilience over time. Mindful practice, patience, and understanding make stronger and more effective relationships possible.

If you feel you are not handling this experience well, share this information with a trusted friend, religious leader, or counselor to enable them to better help you.

An abbreviated summary of the stages of the Emotional Cycle of Deployment (DoD):

- *Anticipation of loss,* leaving behind the familiar, family and friends, routines, comforts; completing necessary to-do lists before deployment.

- *Detachment and withdrawal,* shifting focus to new realities. This helps the reality sink in, so don't take it as rejection.

- *Emotional disorganization,* finding the path to new roles, responsibilities, and support resources; relying on a unit readiness officer for information; and understanding OPSEC.

- *Recovery and stabilization,* establishing new routines, purpose, goals, and successes to manage the time apart; finding new support networks and new ways to support.

- *Anticipation of homecoming,* understanding that everyone has changed, some have grown into new experiences, others are anxious about unresolved issues that existed before separation.

- *Renegotiating the marriage contract* (for married Marines); parents must be patient and respect the couple's space.

- *Reintegration and stabilization,* getting back to "normal" or adjusting to a "new normal," reintegrating effectively;

restoring old relationships and roles; moving forward to set new goals or paths.

Emergencies and Official Information

While the official title varies by unit, deployment readiness co-ordinators (DRC) are reliable points of contact for parents during deployment. Ask your Marine to grant permission for you to have access to this communication resource and to include you in the preparation (pre-deployment) phase of the deployment, to enable you to provide greater support.

For you to be contacted in the event of an emergency with your Marine, your name must appear on their Record of Emergency Data (RED) card. If your Marine is wounded, ill, or injured the person who will be contacted is the person listed on their RED card. Your Marine should update their RED card any time next of kin, addresses, or phone numbers change.

If your Marine is wounded, ill, or injured, or in the event of death, the Marine Corps follows strict rules and regulations regarding notifying next of kin. Notification ranges from a phone call for less-serious situations to a formal official visit by a Marine in person to deliver the news of a Marine's passing.

Before he was married, I asked my son to make a list of his critical personal information—social security number, online usernames and passwords, driver's license number, bank cards, etc. He sealed this information in an envelope, and I assured him I would only open in case of an emergency. You may want to do the same, especially if your Marine is single or does not have family members close by. Protect this critical information; put it in a very secure place.

Operational Security (OPSEC)

Understanding and maintaining operational security is essential to your Marine's safety. Set up healthy and safe communication boundaries for yourself and your family.

The old wartime expression, "Loose lips sink ships," is true.

Practice caution and privacy with your words and posts. Critical information to protect may include military activities or capabilities, troop or ship movements, temporary duty locations, even flight schedules. Be cautious about where, with whom, and how you discuss this information. Social media, internet blogs, and chat rooms are not safe places to reveal this type of information. You can't be certain who else will receive it. Determined individuals may collect and share data from cordless and cellular phones, and even baby monitors. Private conversations conducted in public may be overheard. If you become aware of anyone making a persistent effort to gather information that seems inappropriate, notify your Marine or the unit readiness officer.

Safe and Effective Communication

Use a variety of communication methods to stay connected with your Marine. Find out if video chat or phone calls are possible. A handwritten letter is a welcome sight when Marines gather to hear, "Mail Call!" Even if your Marine may not be able to access email right away, a positive note waiting in their inbox when they can check is a great way to cheer them on. The "pay as you go" service, Sandboxx.us, is a reliable and quick commercial communication app to send digital letters and photos to your Marine.

Care packages are an amazing way to show your love and support. Though surprise goody packages are fun to receive, check in with your Marine to find out what they desperately want or most need when far from home. That might be favorite snacks, substantial socks, foot powder, or deodorant. Whatever it is, make time to send off that package. You are their access to the few precious commodities they can get through the mail during deployment.

Again consider that some Marines in the unit may not have strong family bonds. When a Marine joins the Corps, they belong to a bigger family, and they need to take care of each other.

One Marine shared, "The best way my family supports me is by sending packages of cookies and treats during the holidays for me to share with the other Marines."

When you do get that special phone call or video chat, be prepared by keeping a list of news or items to share so you will use this brief time wisely.

A mother who has supported her Marine and his family through three tours to Iraq, two tours on Marine expeditionary units (MEUs), and four accompanied overseas assignments provides these words of wisdom:

> I have learned to not wait for phone calls or set any expectations. However, when he does call, there is no good time of day or bad time of day: I answer the phone. I try to get the feel of what frame of mind he is in, because I want him to leave our conversation feeling connected and refueled. He is not just a Marine—he is my son. He is a brother, uncle, and grandson. I have learned to gauge when to tell him unfortunate news. For example, his grandfather died during his second tour in Iraq. He deserved to be aware of what was happening at home, and I knew he compartmentalized things well. However, I am also fully aware that when service members are in a combat zone, all their personality traits are amplified. I have worked at stepping back and just listening when he feels like sharing.

The dynamic of your relationship with your Marine, and the calls you share together while they are away, may also shift if other family members are in the picture, such as a spouse or kids. I had to accept that my Marine put his spouse first for phone calls, and I encouraged him to prioritize his relationship with his own children. He needed to kindle those relationships before us. If that meant his dad and I were last in line for phone calls or communications, that was how it needed to be.

Reintegration

When your Marine returns from their deployment, the celebration of their reunion can take many forms that may or may not directly include you as a parent. Also be aware that reintegration can be even more difficult for a family than the deployment itself. Your Marine may or may not be able to visit you. Be open to if and when visiting your Marine may be appropriate. No matter how your reunion takes place, allow your Marine the space and grace to slowly adjust to the world around them again.

Your Marine's spouse and children can take advantage of Families Overcoming Under Stress (FOCUS) at their installation. The FOCUS program and other counseling services are designed to keep families supported, strengthened, and resilient. Many rely on extra support from extended family during deployments, so it's good to know the resources if you feel your Marine or their family needs extra help.

Special Duty Assignments—CONUS

Though many jobs in the Marine Corps send Marines to other parts of the world, your Marine's special duties can occur within the continental United States (CONUS) too. When Marines are not working in their primary MOS, supporting the operational forces, they may be assigned jobs away from their familiar bases, yet within the US. Though serving closer to home, due to their job duties, it may feel similar to being deployed for an unpredictable time—what Marines call a "day-on, stay-on" experience.

Know and respect that your Marine chose to compete for this special duty or opportunity and they passed very rigorous requirements, difficult academic standards, and physical training to be selected for this job. The challenge to go above and beyond, to be the best of the best, requires additional training, separation, and sacrifice. Their success will be impacted by the kind of support and level of understanding their families give them. Many say they depend on the support of family to keep them motivated.

One Marine highlighted this well:

> Do not make the Marine feel guilty if they do
> not respond to calls or texts right away. There are
> no guarantees that they can attend Sunday dinners,

weekend visits, or family events, even if they live close by. Holidays are workdays. Keep me in your heart and thoughts and prayers that I can perform my duties and honor those I am called to serve.

My advice during these types of special assignments is to simply ask, "How can I help you, your spouse, or your children?" They will really appreciate any support and attention you offer. Feel proud that your Marine was selected to serve in this special way.

Following are a few examples where a Marine is chosen from a field of well-qualified competitors. The job rests solely on that Marine to perform in a manner and to a standard requiring special attention. The commitment to duty is one of a Marine's most important values, which makes this person the best of the best!

Recruiting Tours

Spending time with a staff of local recruiters took me back to the days when my husband served in a recruiting tour. As a spouse and young mother of two, I hardly saw him. I counted the days until he could spend a few precious hours with us on a Sunday.

Recruiters refer to a mission as the number of Marine contracts they are required to write, averaging one to two new recruits per month. If your Marine serves a recruiting tour, they will likely have to make hundreds of phone calls and work round the clock, including weekends, to find potential applicants ages seventeen to twenty-five. Not all contracts they bring in will be approved; applicants must meet physical and academic requirements plus clear background checks. It takes many appointments and interviews with each applicant and their family to get one contract per month. Sometimes the Corps needs very specific qualities in new recruits, making the contracting process even more challenging.

All told, a recruiter typically works seventy-five hours per week! After all that, a recruiter only gets credit for a contract if the person completes initial boot camp or OCS training successfully.

Recruiting is an incredibly challenging tour, with high stress, late nights, weekend and holiday work, all at risk to personal and marital relationships. The rewards usually include the choice of the next duty station or assignment, offered for a job well done.

Drill Instructors and Series Commanders

Drill fields at boot camp or OCS are staffed by Marines who compete and are chosen for this assignment because of their exceptional standards and accomplishments in their primary occupational fields. Their day begins before sunup and ends after sundown seven days a week, for three to four months at a time. In addition to training, supervising, and evaluating the recruits and candidates, they adapt and adjust a behind-the-scenes operational schedule, while maintaining their own physical and leadership standards of excellence, which they model for those in their care.

Casualty Assistance and Funeral Honors

These are the Marines whose presence is on public display during the most difficult times. Their duties speak to the level of compassion and care Marines feel toward their fellow Marines. Their dedication to duty and standards of excellence honor those they serve. The time and commitment to serve requires special attention to detail, as well as being present at the request of the units and families they serve.

Marine Bands

Other demanding jobs worth mentioning are those held by musician Marines, who audition to perform in Marine bands around the country. They spend many hours practicing and drilling, plus time on the road, on tour, or responding to requests for ceremonial activities. Those hours and days add up. This job could be a permanent, professional position in Washington, DC, as a member of "The President's Own" band or "The Commandant's Own" US Marine Drum and Bugle Corps. Other Marine bands draw from local Marine talent. Their musical duties are performed on a parade deck, in a community parade, or at special ceremonies. In some circumstances, band members have been called into combat duties, to deploy and carry weapons, not instruments.

Enlisted and Officer Aides to General Officers

Marines selected for these duties allow the general officers they serve to do their jobs on a minute-by-minute, hour-by-hour, day-by-day basis, with precision. These positions require them to independently support the scheduling, meal planning, proper uniform standards, and housing details, anywhere in the world, where the general may be required to work. Aides also make spending and budget decisions, and ensure legal issues and regulations pass scrutiny at every level of the law.

Special Duty Stations Around the Globe—OCONUS

Some assignments take a Marine to other parts of the world, outside the continental US (OCONUS). Marines are constantly on the move in every climate, from the hottest desert or jungle to the coldest seas or mountaintops, and every imaginable place around the globe. Some orders require the Marine to go alone; others include their spouse and children.

The potential for travel or living overseas is a great pull for military members. When a Marine is sent to a remote location thousands of miles away, different family support is needed.

Whether your Marine is activated for a deployment, accompanied overseas tour, or shorter temporary duty assignment, it helps to understand what the family will face with their loved one overseas. You can help in a variety of powerful and positive ways.

Overseas Permanent Change of Station

Deployments are not the only way your Marine will go out and experience the world. If a Marine receives overseas orders, they may be gone for one, two, three, or more years! Some Marines seek out overseas assignments, especially if they can take their families.

A Marine spouse shared her hope to go abroad:

> My husband and I both grew up as military brats and spent several years overseas ourselves. Now as parents, we were able to provide the same experiences for our children.

Others may be surprised by orders or enter them for specific reasons, as one spouse shares about a tour to South Korea:

> Korea was not even on our list of places we thought we could go, but my Marine wanted to go overseas and believed the change in his MOS would be good for his career. My daughter and I joined him.

Whether the family is looking forward to overseas orders or not, one thing is for certain: heavy preparation is in order!

Preparation for OCONUS

Not all orders provide the opportunity for family members to join their Marine in another country. Single Marines and married Marines accepting an unaccompanied tour will receive with their orders an allotment for personal items, housing, and information about benefits for their family not accompanying them. These logistical requirements are numerous prior to leaving for an overseas assignment. Single Marines may need to store personal items or vehicles stateside. Depending on one's rank or job, a vehicle may not be allowed. But this is far less complicated compared to a Marine who has the option to take their spouse or children.

Accompanied orders means the Marine's immediate family will move overseas with them. The items a family is allowed to bring overseas are more limited than for moves within the US.

It can be frustrating to downsize and figure out exactly what resources another country may or may not have. Remind your Marine they are capable. Here are the most likely terms the family will encounter:

Unaccompanied baggage (UAB): A limited, small poundage allotment will be sent via airplane. Furniture is not allowed, with few exceptions such as folding baby cribs. The family will want to pack essential living items (e.g., dishes, sheets); a few favorite toys or books for young children; uniforms and essential clothing for each family member; and important paperwork (hand carry). It may take up to three months or more for the rest of the household goods shipment, which arrives by boat.

Household goods/effects (HHG/E): Whatever the family decides to move will take a fairly lengthy time to get to the duty station as it is generally shipped from a dock on a large cargo ship. The family will need to determine if housing will include furnished apartments. Many overseas locations do, which enables families to move less weight around the world. Since Marine families are moving out of the area as new families are moving in, there is often an opportunity to swap or purchase used goods for the few years they will be living in the country.

Non-temp storage (NTS): The family will say goodbye to the rest of their stuff as it is hauled into storage. If approved, storage will be paid for, but the belongings may or may not be stored in a temperature-controlled climate. This is very basic storage, where the family will place what they believe they can live without for the length of orders. It is not recommended to store or ship valuables or sentimental items that are not easily replaced. This may be an area where you as a parent can offer to pick up and store special items if practical.

Personally owned vehicle (POV) shipment: Your Marine may be allowed to store or move a vehicle, or they may need to consider selling it before they go. The country they are moving to may drive on the opposite side of the road, for example, in which case they would need to get a proper vehicle upon arrival to the country—just one of the many fun quirks of overseas life!

On the plane: Some overseas moves rate heavy baggage. This means the orders will allow up to seventy pounds per suitcase when flying, and a larger number of bags per person. Depending on the airline, the family may have to pay for heavy baggage and get reimbursed later.

Pro-gear: Your Marine will be able to claim a certain amount of their military gear as pro-gear, meaning it does not count against the overall weight allotment.

Vaccinations: When given overseas orders, your Marine and their family will need medical clearance for the country they are moving to. This could mean new vaccinations. One family that has been stationed in Korea, Africa, and South America gained several rounds of shots for rabies, Japanese encephalitis, typhoid, and yellow fever. The vaccination costs are covered and done to protect the Marine and their family while carrying out overseas orders.

Housing: Depending on the post, the family may have the choice to move on base or off base. A family stationed in Seoul, South Korea, said:

> Our housing was very comfortable overseas. I
> was thankful we chose to live on base, as I had a great
> feeling of support with fellow military neighbors. I
> also enjoyed having amenities I was used to, such as
> a full-size oven, and washer and dryer!

A family is allowed to accompany the Marine with Security Guard orders if the Marine is of a certain rank or job, and if the area is deemed safe for families. They will be placed in embassy housing, which again will either be in a gated community or out in town. An MSG spouse stationed in the Democratic Republic of the Congo, Africa, wished that her concerned family stateside understood their housing better. She explained:

> I try and tell them that we live out in town just
> like the locals and this concept seems to be confusing
> to my family. The MSG program takes care of its
> people very well. When we live out in town, it is
> because they have found the safest place to live in
> town and ensure the proper security measures are in
> place within your home.

Moving overseas is a labor-intensive process; it can also be an emotionally draining process. Parents can support and assist in many ways. Some days, a simple phone call will suffice. One spouse noted:

> As we were moving from Hawaii to Morocco, my
> daughter's grandparents would call when I was trying
> to sort the house. I would set up the video chat on

the desk, and my toddler would happily watch them read books to her! Even though they couldn't be there in person to aid us, they provided international on-call babysitting, and that was more than enough to get us through that stressful time.

Care Package Ideas

Plan to have a few care packages ready to ship, so that as soon as the family arrives in their new foreign land, they have comforts of home on the way. Send special food items to your Marine that do not exist or are expensive to purchase in the local economy. One grandparent sent macaroni and cheese boxes, playdough, and children's books. Another grandparent sent chunky peanut butter, taco shells, paper sandwich bags for school lunches, and ten pounds of Southern-style grits. Comfort food was a welcome surprise for the Marine and his family. Be sure to check the requirements for shipping food to your Marine's country; avoid perishable food in case your package takes a while to arrive.

Living Overseas and Making Visits a Priority

Overseas accompanied tours are incredible opportunities to see the world, but they are not free from hardship. One of the toughest strains on the Marine and their family members is the cost to travel back to the US to see family, which can be thousands of dollars. The family is faced with a hard choice: go back to the States for visits, or use their paychecks to travel the world while they have the chance.

A Marine family serving back-to-back tours in Hawaii and Okinawa, Japan, had this to say:

> We're lucky to have family who understand our situation and that being stationed overseas is an opportunity for our family. They are very supportive and encourage us to travel and see the world while we are in Japan. However, they do have a hard time understanding how difficult it can be to fly home. We

live in Japan, but our family is scattered up and down the east coast of the United States. So not only do we need to buy five very expensive plane tickets, we have to then travel around state to state to check everyone off our list. It's not that we don't want to visit; it's that sometimes we just can't. Not having someone resent the fact that you're so far away is the best way to support a military family.

One Marine and his family knew that with four children they could not return to the States on their tour. Instead, their parents came to see them and were present for the fourth child's birth in Japan. That visit was life-giving for the Marine family, enabling the Marine's spouse to rest after the birth and giving them extra hands at home with their other children.

Some family and friends are eager to schedule a visit overseas and travel to exciting new places with their Marine family. Sharing an overseas experience is an awesome chance to see the world with new eyes. One Marine found himself laughing with his father-in-law, as they blazed down the roads of Africa together. "Did you ever think we would end up here?!" The answer from them both was a resounding, "No, but we are glad we're here!"

Depending on the circumstances of the tour, living abroad can be a lonely experience. Similar to a deployment, the pressure of time constraints and being thousands of miles away are eased by getting creative with how to stay in touch. If you cannot visit, try phone calls, letters, and emails. Find time for video chats. Keep investing in your Marine, even from far away.

Be considerate and intentional with how you share news. Whether your news is about an exciting accomplishment or a serious health crisis, your Marine family will appreciate you sharing it with them directly first (keeping in mind their time zone) before posting on social media, for example. They already feel far away from you; simple gestures like including them first in your communications will go a long way in helping them feel close to home.

If you aren't able to spend time in person, the years flying by between visits can be especially hard for grandparents. A Marine's spouse in Japan with two children and a third on the way said:

> I sympathize for our parents and the loss they're going through. They are a truly brave bunch to be able to say goodbye so many times, not knowing how long it'll be until we see them again.

One Marine and his family served four consecutive overseas tours, totaling eight years away from the US:

> We do not take much for granted anymore. We remind one another how lucky we are to have each other, to have seen the world, and to have made home wherever we are. Our first child was born overseas and has grown up overseas.
>
> It is heartwarming to us that our parents get on the plane. They come to where we are. And when they can't, video calls make all the difference. On a recent trip back to the United States, we were collecting our luggage and Grandma walked into baggage claim. Our daughter was then three years old and had not seen her grandmother for six months in person, yet she ran straight into her arms. She knows who her family is, and that is because we have worked to form those bonds. Love is love, no matter how many thousands of miles away.

Travel Preparation

My mother's bucket list included wanting to visit us in every duty station. We were excited for the opportunity to share our experiences with my parents and make unique memories. For example, when we were stationed in Italy, we all visited the birthplace of my father's family in Sicily. We met relatives we did not know we had! My father was not in the best of health at the time, so I planned ahead to locate the nearest hospital and emergency numbers in case we needed them. The trip was a joyous event, and those memories have lasted a lifetime in our family.

If you choose to visit your Marine, traveling overseas requires preparation. A pre-travel checklist might include items such as:

- Discuss plans with your Marine to determine if the trip is possible. If you plan to surprise them, they may not be there, and it will be you who is surprised and disappointed.

- Obtain or update passports well in advance of the trip.

- Check special vaccination or medical requirements for that specific country, and consider any medications you need to take with you.

- Purchase overseas health insurance and travel insurance to protect yourself and your family.

- Consider State Department restrictions and OPSEC awareness in your travel planning.

- Search for the types of hotel accommodations and transportation you can expect in the country—yes, donkeys and camels are sometimes on the list.

- Be realistic when planning your budget. Consider currency exchange rate fluctuations and unanticipated expenses.

Marine Security Guard

The Marine Security Guard (MSG) program is an amazing, career-defining and life-experience-building opportunity. Single enlisted Marines (up to the rank of sergeant) may serve as watchstanders to protect US Embassies, Consulates, and other diplomatic missions in foreign countries. Staff sergeants and above may serve as a detachment commander. The program is intense and the hours are long. Marines might serve two or three 12-month posts in up to three different countries around the world.

Marines are trained at a special school, at Marine Corps Embassy Security Group (MCESG), Quantico, Virginia, prior to their first MSG assignment. The day before graduation is set aside to provide parents and family members gathered at the school with specific resources about this new assignment. Similar to most deploying units, the program's final day is full of information, but it also adds a special glimpse of the lifestyle of MSG watchstanders and the detachment commander, and their unique relationship with the US Department of State.

A unit readiness officer is the point of contact for families, serving at the headquarters level in Virginia and linked to a community liaison officer at an embassy.

A Marine who served in Brussels, Belgium; Kathmandu, Nepal; and Rabat, Morocco, had this to stay about the program and how his family supported him over his three years across the globe:

> The reason I joined the MSG program was to explore the world and experience a different culture outside of our country. My family handled my absence well as I had already been away from home since the age of eighteen, with only a few visits back and forth before I was on MSG. I know my mom is really proud of me, no matter where I go.

That same Marine's mother met her son in Paris during the Thanksgiving holiday, bringing an entire Thanksgiving feast in her suitcase! She cooked up the dinner to share with her Marine and his fellow Marines on the program. They feasted and toasted their gratitude that year as the city of lights glowed around them.

Not all Marines on the program are able to have family visit, but this does not diminish their relationship. One Marine said:

> My family and I constantly stay in contact, they send care packages, and most importantly, they keep me in their daily prayers.

Another Marine who would not be visiting family back home on his three-year MSG tour received a memorable care package. His family asked him what he needed, and he said, "Send me some of Arizona, and I'll be happy!" They packaged up a special pair of cowboy boots that he had received for high school graduation. He shared:

> A lot of my favorite memories as well as part of who I am are in those boots. The boots came, some menudo, and a few shirts that had my hometown written on them. That was the best.

As a parent, you can send your love anywhere in the world! Your Marine has an amazing skill set and is trained for whatever mission lies ahead, in any corner of the globe. Parents can stand up alongside their Marine in their own ways by providing ongoing encouragement and support.

Chapter Three

Semper Family

MARINES USE THE WORD "SEMPER" in all sorts of expressions. Of Latin origin, *semper* means always or ever. In this case, being a "Semper Family" is cause to celebrate—your Marine's family is expanding to include a new spouse and possibly children. This will bring joy and complexity to your relationship with your Marine. Even if you have been their primary supportive relationship, their new life partner will take on much of that role going forward. As you figure out this new journey together, keep in mind another Marine phrase, "Semper Gumby," meaning always flexible!

Marriage

I have three married children. My relationship with each one is as different as each of their unique personalities. My attitude is that I always want to be helpful, not hurtful. Developing a good relationship with a child's new spouse takes time, Marine or not.

Military marriage has all the same adjustments of a civilian marriage, including becoming a new member of a spouse's family. But it also means adjusting to a new military culture together. At times, that can be particularly hard on couples.

The role of the Marine's spouse is critical. The promise to love and honor, in good times and bad, takes on a different meaning when the person they marry also takes an oath to protect and defend their country against all enemies foreign and domestic! As

41

a life partner in this journey, a spouse shares the challenges, successes, and rewards. They provide continuity in the family relationship by raising the children and keeping a Marine's parents informed. Spouses are key in sustaining the relationship between the grandparents and grandchildren, especially when a Marine is deployed or not able to reach out as easily to personally share news or updates on recent activities. With each relocation, deployment cycle, and reintegration, your Marine's spouse will likely develop a special relationship with you and their other relatives.

One spouse shared:

> My parents have been lovingly married for almost forty years. I truly look to them as a wonderful example of how to sustain both love and friendship over the course of a lifetime. However, I had to learn the hard way after marrying my Marine that my parents no longer held all the answers. We had to make a switch between parent-daughter relationships to parent-friend relationships. They are not military, and never will fully understand the inner challenges our family has had to face. I believe we all work to understand life through our own experiences—and they have never had to experience a deployment or the joyful but painful reintegration period after my Marine comes home from a deployment. They have not moved around the world or needed to put their kids in new schools, or start new jobs, or unpack a house over and over again.
>
> That said, our parents have found ways to support our marriage, and that has been very appreciated by both my husband and me. They have shown up to where we are around the world. They have given us (and encouraged us) to take nights away from our children when they visit or when we visit them. One of the most important gifts they

have given us is to encourage our hearts, even when they have been stressed and hardened. Life is hard enough; you need a cheering section—they continue to cheer on our marriage.

Whether the marriage begins at a full military wedding with a healthy rump-tap from a sword after "I do" or as a rushed but exhilarating race to elope before a deployment, your support for your Marine and their spouse on their marriage journey will go a long way for their well-being and yours.

Planning for the Wedding

A wedding day is a big deal for many couples and their families. Different cultures and traditions determine how a wedding is performed. The big decision for your Marine is whether or not they will wear their uniform. Some Marine couples want to focus on the union of husband and wife, while others see wearing a uniform as a symbol of the added union of the couple and the Corps.

If your Marine couple wants a traditional military wedding, the Marine Corps Association offers a comprehensive guide with complete details. This resource is especially helpful for you as a parent if your Marine is not available to answer the many specific questions you may have.

Another important consideration is asking vendors about event insurance in case the wedding needs to be postponed or canceled due to military obligations or orders. The expense of a wedding is a big investment. Having a plan B or C or D will help make the wedding day and the honeymoon run smoothly.

Eloping

Due to the quick tempo of military life, elopements are more common than a long-planned wedding ceremony. Some lucky couples may get to have both. One reason eloping is common is because a marriage license issued by any justice of the peace is the only item necessary in the administrative procedure to obtain an ID card for a new spouse. This entitles the couple to receive extra funds and moving support, which are not offered to a single Marine with an unmarried life partner. When a Marine receives orders to their first duty station after the initial training requirements, eloping allows their spouse to be listed on those orders.

One couple took advantage of this option and eloped while the Marine was finishing the School of Infantry training. After graduation, they began married life and still enjoyed a well-planned church wedding and honeymoon. The wedding gifts were packed and delivered to their first duty station as legitimate military "household goods" from the bride's hometown. Planning ahead enabled them to start their new life together with the items they needed to start married life in their first home.

Another Marine spouse remembers her elopement fondly:

> My husband proposed over a family holiday in Ohio, and seven days later we were married in Colorado! Five days after that, he boarded a plane to Iraq, and I was hired to dance for Carnival Cruise Lines. Nine months later, we met back up in California and finally started our first year of marriage together. It was pretty crazy, but it was also our choice, and one that was made easier as our families supported us in their own ways.
>
> After his proposal, he mentioned how we should get married before he deployed. At first, I said, "No way!" I dreamed of the big white wedding and my dad walking me down the aisle. But we had already gone through two previous deployments together and, with this one, he wanted to protect me. Saying yes to a marriage proposal does not just mean romance, (although let's hope that's a big part of it!), it means being recognized by the military as a lawful dependent. After our union, I was now his beneficiary. This meant I was covered by medical health insurance, and we could receive separation

pay while he was deployed. Every little bit helped, and our parents also encouraged us. They sat down with us and said, "'We know you love each other, and we are excited for you to get married—even if it means an elopement. However, we want to share in your joy. Please promise us that we can have a party for you when all this is said and done. We want to celebrate with you."

This helped me have more peace in my heart—and we did have a second wedding! We held off on exchanging our wedding rings until we repeated our vows in front of our family, and the big wedding was just a year and a half after our elopement! The wedding was everything I hoped for and more, we were just already married! We always laugh looking back, as it was such a stress-free, beautiful day with our family and friends. I'm glad we married when we did, and I am glad our families made sure we stuck to our dreams of another wedding after.

While an elopement *and* a wedding after may be unconventional, it can work. A marriage is about love, and it is also a binding contract with financial and legal implications. Your Marine may want to protect their future spouse and give them access to their benefits, especially if they will soon deploy. This may mean a hasty wedding up front and a more traditional party with friends and family later. Support your Marine and their spouse, even if it is disappointing to not be able to attend the initial wedding ceremony.

International Spouses

Marines can be stationed all over the world, so it's not unusual for them to fall in love outside the US or marry a service member from another country. This brings new challenges, from the joining of two people with two very different cultures to the interviewing and documenting process about their union required for the Marine's command. While paperwork, interviews, and dealing with the legality of marrying a foreign national can be a lengthy process, it is for the protection of both parties.

It is incredibly brave to leave your family and natural culture and language behind. A Korean spouse reflected on her journey:

> It was definitely a huge change. I was/am challenged every single day to learn a different language, culture, and what to expect with life as a military spouse. Getting married to a foreign national Marine was very tough until we actually settled down into our life together. First I felt very confused about myself. I met and married my husband who is a Marine when I was in Korea. Before I moved to the United States, I actually had no idea how much my life would change.
>
> In Korea I was very independent and able to handle my life pretty well, like a normal adult. For example, I graduated from school, I had a job, and making friends was very simple, as was getting groceries or shopping without anyone's help. But after getting married, what I knew or had for my life in Korea was all over. I had to take my husband to a doctor's appointment with me because I couldn't understand simple medical terms that the doctor was using. I felt so humiliated!
>
> Until I overcame this dark period, I felt so lost and trapped. In that time, I learned to never question anything with my husband and his job, I learned to just accept it. He sometimes deploys for half a year. He can't tell me why he has to go, how long, or sometimes where he goes. I cannot ask what happened or what is going on at his job. When he is lucky, he will not be gone that long, but he still could be gone months at a time. Nothing is sure. I had so many questions at the beginning for him: *What is*

*going on at work? What do you do? So what is your
job as a Marine? When do we move? How long do we
have here? …*

Sometimes I feel very isolated. People in my
home country do not understand what I'm going
through. I have a duty to protect my husband and
his work, which is sometimes more secretive. But
my friends and family always want me to give them
answers that I cannot. So I have learned to not tell
them, or only let them know what is going on at the
last minute.

I've met lots of military spouses from different
countries. We all have our own issues, but most of
them are going through very tough times for most
of the reasons I mentioned here. My husband and I
have never regretted our decision to get married, but
it's very tough.

This spouse also shared what a blessing it was for both families
to attend their wedding in Korea. They had a traditional Korean
wedding and a more Western-style service directly after, meeting
the needs of both cultures for both sets of parents.

Parents can support the foreign national spouse in respectful ways such as being patient if the new spouse is trying to learn
the English language. Learning simple phrases in their language
is a great first step, as is learning more about their favorite dishes or customs. Exchanging information and respectful curiosity
for each other's home cultures can create bonds for a lifetime and
are perfect family-building and fun activities. Marines often share
meals and traditions and learn some of the native language during
deployments, so it will be helpful for you to learn a few items too.

A foreign spouse may not be able to drive yet, or even work in
America, so there is a big learning curve for all involved.

This next couple had an easier transition. The Marine's spouse
is German. The Marine shared:

When my wife and I got married, I would not say that it was extraordinarily hard. My wife at the time already had a green card; she spoke great English and had been living in the US for several years. The hardest part was running into some issues with my security clearance. The documents I submitted were lost and not submitted. It took several months and about forty pages of paperwork to get it all resolved, but it did all eventually work out. As far as the marriage ceremony itself, we'd both been married previously and decided to go with something a little unconventional. We were married by an Elvis at a drive-through wedding chapel in Las Vegas! My wife was six months pregnant at the time.

My wife was naturalized as a US citizen seven years later on the battleship Missouri at Pearl Harbor in Hawaii. Getting her citizenship was a complicated and somewhat expensive process, but my wife went after it and achieved it.

Since every country has its own requirements, couples may need to figure out citizenship or documentation on their own.

Re-engaged (Life After the Wedding)

Showing support for newlyweds bonds new families together in a very special way. The early months and years are spent getting to know each other as well as establishing their own traditions and blending each other's family traditions.

Setting boundaries respectfully is an important gift to share and discuss as a new family. To find the sweet spot that honors everyone's relationships, both sides of the family need to work on ways to stay in touch with family news, celebrate special occasions, and honor family relationships. A few ways to support each other:

- Remember birthdays, anniversaries, holidays, Mother's Day, and Father's Day with calls, cards, or letters.

- Send thank-you notes when you receive packages or gifts—a simple text or a picture of you with the gift is a nice touch. It's never too late to say thank you!

- Set special times or days for regular phone or video visits, especially to stay connected to grandchildren.

- Discuss ahead of time what you will do in moments of crisis: accidents, illness, or death of family members.

- Discuss how visits for holidays, vacations (military leave), time between station-to-station moves, and so forth are going to be determined. This decision has many variables, so military members and families may ask for patience and understanding during these times.

- Consider having hometown families travel to see the Marine and family—this can be an exciting adventure!

- Agree on a mediator—family, friend, counselor, or religious adviser—to help work out misunderstandings if these keep you from communicating. Don't let hard feelings linger! Avoid situations where anyone feels misunderstood, left out, or ignored.

Extra Support

The Department of Defense offers numerous resources for military marriages through classes and retreats on each base installation, designed to improve and reconnect couple relationships.

Sometimes the strain of military life weighs heavily on couples. This is true in normal assignments; add deployment or overseas assignments and military couples may need extra time to work on their relationship or to take a break from the everyday stress.

This couple was stationed together on the Marine Security Group in North Africa:

> We moved to Africa right after the birth of
> our child and after two very lengthy back-to-back
> deployments. It was a blessing to be together, but we

went from one high-operational tempo into another. Add the stress of being overseas in a country, and we were not in a great chapter of our union! We had a lot of work to do on our marriage and had to do it in a strenuous place. One of the best moments for us was when my in-laws came out to stay with us for six weeks. We were in a rough spot with one another at the time, and they encouraged us to take a trip together, just the two of us.

The generosity of their spirit in pushing us out the door together, and the bravery they showed us in staying in our home, alone, and with our daughter for a week in Africa showed us the true love and support a family can provide. We never would have left our daughter with a sitter for that long in a foreign country, but knowing that her grandparents were there to see to her care gave us the freedom to go. We enjoyed our own mini-retreat, traveling together for six nights and seven days. It gave us a chance to talk, to see each other in this new stage of life together, and to breathe life back into our marriage. I'll never forget that gift of time they granted us. We are now on track in our marriage and excitedly looking forward to the future.

It might not be every grandparent's ideal situation—navigating Africa so their Marine and spouse can have a life-giving trip—however, it is an example of how volunteering to watch a grandchild or stepping in and providing a little relief and space for the couple can make a huge difference in their marriage. Whether you come from a family history in the military, or this is a new path for you to navigate, providing support for your Marine and their spouse, regardless of where they live, is a choice you can make to impact them positively for a lifetime.

Effective communication is near the top of the list of issues that concern military families. The time it takes to deal with long-distance relationships, commitment to duties and responsibilities, and communication skills that are still developing in a new relationship, can contribute to increased stress and tension in an environment where much is out of a Marine's control. Growing strong, healthy, lasting relationships is possible when families support each other and work together.

Chapter Four

Long-Distance Grandparents

BECOMING A GRANDPARENT is one of life's greatest joys. It also shifts family roles and dynamics. Your child becomes a parent, your grandchild's parent. You'll want to understand everyone's expectations of one another and be willing to shift those expectations. Whether it was our first grandchild or our last, each pregnancy was a long-distance experience for us. We tried to offer support though video chats, care packages, and attending baby showers, when possible. Being on the sidelines felt a bit unnatural because being supportive grandparents was very important to us. Our greatest concern was that our grandchildren would not know us or feel a connection to us. Fortunately, our fears have not come to pass. Now, many years later, being a long-distance grandparent has not lessened or diminished our relationship with any of them. We just had to be creative to forge those special bonds.

Chances to interact in person with your grandchildren may be limited for a variety of reasons, namely because they are a military kid! Constant relocations, financial travel restrictions, busy schedules, and deployments can make family dynamics stressful. Good communication and teamwork are key to helping families stay close regardless of the physical distance between them.

Birth of a Grandchild

Even if you've already been promoted to grandparent status, prepare for a different experience this time around. Being a grandparent of your Marine's children will carry its own set of challenges. You may think you can step into the new role once the baby is born; but often due to the Marine's mission, grandparents-to-be need to provide support several months before the birth. Your emotional support is critically important in many ways.

Here is a beautiful story of a family entering their fourth deployment together and welcoming their first child:

> My husband and I discussed which I would rather do: be pregnant alone or have the baby alone. These seemed like insane and yet totally normal questions to ask. Insane because I may never have had to answer this question outside of military life, but normal because the United States Marine Corps is our life, and we knew going in that we would not have what we deemed a "normal" family life. Neither my husband nor I came from military families. We grew up in the same place for eighteen years, with our own grandparents just miles down the road.
>
> As we entered parenthood in the military, we had to redefine what our first-child experiences would look like. It started with my Marine deploying and, five days after he left, I discovered I was pregnant! It was an astounding joy, but I could not get a hold of him to tell him as he was en route with the Marine Expeditionary Unit. Instead, I called my best friend. We jumped for joy together in unison, though we were thousands of miles apart, with me in Hawaii and her in New York City!
>
> I wanted to keep the pregnancy private aside from telling my best friend, waiting to tell anyone else until I could tell my husband the happy news.

But a few weeks into the pregnancy, I started bleeding and believed a miscarriage could be on the way. This was two days before my parents were coming to keep me company for a month during the deployment. I had to call and tell them what they were walking into: either an imminent sadness or the hope that our baby was staying with us. They came to my doctor's appointment with me, and we all got to see the first glimpses of their new granddaughter together. She was fine. I was reassured as my mom and dad held my hand (and my hair back) during the queasy moments of my first trimester.

After they left, my mother-in-law flew out in my last trimester and aided in setting up the nursery and registering for baby gifts. She even rubbed my back as I cried in the baby supply store as I watched other pregnant couples wandering around together, getting to do all the things I thought I would be doing with my husband. It was a bittersweet time when I think all our family realized this pregnancy was such a blessing, but also a point where I needed to give myself a lot of grace to let go of the expectations of doing it all alongside my partner. I had to count my gratitude for those who showed up to support me and share, when I could, the delight of our baby with my husband.

One of the smartest things my family did was encourage me to have the doctor email the gender of our baby to my husband. He did not get to come to any of the other appointments with me, but he was the first to find out that our baby was a girl! It was a really special way to include him in the pregnancy.

This couple had some tough chats about family matters once the deployed Marine arrived home. He made it back in time for the birth. His spouse was thirty-six weeks into her pregnancy when he finally arrived home in the beginning of December, with the baby due in January. The couple had an honest conversation with their families that they did not want any visitors for Christmas or until after the baby was born. They saw it as the last time to cherish their marriage as two people before three. They asked their parents to respect that, and they did. The spouse remembers:

> If I would do anything different after having our daughter, it would be to have our family visit sooner! I know it may not be the best choice for everyone, but—wow—did I not realize how tough having a newborn is! With my husband still having to work long hours in preparation for another deployment, I was exhausted. My in-laws finally coming out when our daughter was four weeks old was completely life-giving! We needed our village around us, helping to cook, clean, and hold our sweet girl!

How to respectfully create and honor healthy boundaries is a choice. When this family discussed family visits with the new grandchild, both sets of grandparents were honest. The mother- and father-in-law wanted to see the baby and their son before the fifth deployment. They also loved helping with newborn baby needs, so they flew out first. The other grandparents chose to come out when the child was four months old, communicating that they preferred to help as the baby was a bit older. Both grandparents sent care packages and made meaningful phone calls.

If further deployments are likely, you may want to discuss with your Marine what your role will be as a grandparent on those upcoming deployments. One Marine family discovered that developing relationships with grandparents was tricky given the distance:

> My spouse and I have always lived away from family (even when we were both children), so our interactions with family have been pretty limited. My mom has been our biggest supporter in all things

grandparent-related. She has traveled to us, wherever we are, for each child's birthday—routinely staying with us for a month at a time; and she continues to do that even while we're overseas. She is great at making sure that even though she doesn't see her grandchildren more than once or twice a year, she forges relationships with them. They video call and write letters. They share their interests in knitting, cooking, and art with her, and they seek her advice.

I think for her, a person who moved away from Ireland in her twenties and never went back, she understands what it is like to live away from family and to work on developing those relationships.

Deployment Births

One of the most challenging situations a military family can face is enduring labor and delivery apart from each other. As hard as it is, many Marine families accept and confront this obstacle as part of their story. While some grandparents might be asked to step in to support the spouse during this time, others may be unable to travel or be present for the delivery.

A seasoned Marine spouse shares:

My husband was present for the birth of our first two children, but he was deployed when the third was born. It was a very challenging pregnancy for me emotionally, because I knew the entire time that he would miss the birth of our child. Luckily, we were able to make some plans in advance that helped me feel more confident about the situation.

First I contacted a doula and asked her to be with me in the room throughout the birth, since I knew no other family members could be there to assist me. I had never used a doula before, but I'm so glad I did in this situation. I used the program Operation Special Delivery, because at the time (during the peak of the Iraq/Afghanistan deployments) they offered free doula services to military spouses. Now there is a reduced military rate designed to make them affordable, while still compensating the doula for their time. In my case, I did not know my doula personally, but she met with me several times during the pregnancy to discuss the birth plan and help put me at ease.

As my due date approached, we remained in contact via text message to discuss contractions and labor signs. When I went into labor, she checked my contraction timing, drove me to the hospital, and helped me answer questions and complete the admission paperwork. She remained with me through the entire procedure, offering emotional and physical support, breathing exercises that helped lower my heart rate, and keeping me informed of my medical options. She also helped hold my phone so I could send messages to my husband about the birth.

In some cases, deployed service members are able to witness their children's birth via internet calls or video apps. My husband didn't have those options at his small base in Afghanistan, but he was granted permission to sit in the communications tent that day and have internet access. So we sent messages through instant messaging, and the doula snapped a photo of our baby as soon as he was born. Having that connection meant so much to me, because it was a challenging birth to get through without my husband by my side.

I had also invited a friend to be present with me in the delivery room. She was a mom of three kids and had a great sense of humor, so I thought her presence would help me. Unfortunately, there was a Category 3 hurricane that struck our town the day I gave birth, so the base was shut down, and she was not allowed access. That's why having a doula proved to be an invaluable resource; without the doula, I would have been completely alone.

This spouse was also wise in how she communicated with her mother about her needs during this pregnancy and birth:

> The other preparations I made during pregnancy helped the birth and recovery period go more smoothly. I asked for help from everyone and was amazed how many people said yes! My mom volunteered to stay with me starting the week of my due date. She assisted with my preschooler and toddler when I was going into labor and stayed home with them for a few days while I was in the hospital. She ended up staying with me for a few weeks afterward, which had stressful moments, but was overall a great blessing. She cooked, helped with laundry, and played with the older kids so I could focus on feeding the baby. She also drove our oldest child to preschool. After my mom went home, I had several meals brought over by friends from my fellow mothers in our playdate group.

Sometimes the best help can come from other military families. Grandparents cannot always stay through a deployment. Bountiful resources are out in the military community and offered on base, but the Marine and their spouse must be willing to ask for assistance. The same Marine spouse and mother mentions:

> Often military units will set up a meal train to provide home-cooked meals to a new mom. I had one neighbor volunteer to cut our grass, and a friend volunteered to deep clean my house. Those gestures meant so much, because they were tasks I couldn't keep up with on my own. There are base resources we used when preparing for earlier births

but, because this was my third, I didn't need them
again. I encourage military families to use any and all
resources available in their area. Giving birth alone is
not easy, and you need all the help you can get!

Grandparents can feel assured that their Marine family has
good local resources available to new parents:

- Every base hospital offers tours of the labor and delivery
  unit, which a pregnant mother can do ahead of the birth.
  Even if the family decides to have their baby off-base,
  each hospital should have the same practices and tours for
  expecting parents.

- A lactation consultant is usually available for free at the
  hospital on base, and bases typically have free breastfeeding
  support groups for new mothers.

- The New Parent Support Program is available for free
  on base, and the program nurses will do home visits for
  infants to answer questions, check their growth, and
  support nursing mothers. The program is particularly
  beneficial for Marine moms returning to work.

Another Marine mom shares:

> I was referred to the New Parent Support
> Program automatically because I had a history
> of depression prior to pregnancy. My program
> counselor met with me as often as I wanted, helped
> educate me on anything I felt like I needed, and
> spoke with me about anything that was bothering
> me. She was really my life support during that time,
> as she was a neutral third party who I could ask
> anything and everything of without feeling silly.

Grandparents can gently remind their Marine of the pletho-
ra of helpful resources available to active-duty family members.
On-base classes help parents prepare for baby care, create a baby
budget, and support a new baby's siblings. Many organizations

also host baby showers for expectant parents. Such resources are helpful during a deployment birth and can help a Marine expecting their first child to wrap their mind around the fact that parenthood is on the way. During the deployment, the Marine has had to focus on the deployment mission and may not have been home during the pregnancy or other preparations.

Marines who return home from deployment a short time before the birth may miss free birth-preparation classes, but can participate in other programs that help new parents reintegrate and prepare for the newest addition to their family. Hiring a doula or private coach in the privacy of their own home can also help a Marine shift their mindset from deployment duty to parent duty.

Supporting Grandchildren During Deployments

The official flower of the military child is the dandelion because the plant can put down roots almost anywhere, and it is nearly impossible to destroy. Military children learn resilience early on and understand that the world is bigger than their own backyard. They are also part of a living history, with service parents enduring deployments and carrying on a military family legacy.

Grandparents play an important role in their grandchildren's lives all the time, but especially during deployments.

The first major area of support to consider is physical proximity: visiting or living close to your grandchild while your Marine is away. Some Marine spouses choose to leave their current post to be closer to family during a deployment. They must weigh the benefits of living with or near hometown families against the legal and financial challenges. For families with on-base housing, moving out for more than thirty days may mean losing their housing, and subletting is not allowed. For those living off base, it may be difficult to be released from a lease, and maintaining rent, utilities, and yard maintenance from afar can get expensive.

When Families Return Home During Deployments

Each of the next two families experienced different moving scenarios during deployment. Though most spouses don't return home, the two spouses presented here did return home and shared that they needed to rely on their local friends and support services for extra help to make their moves possible. They each gained knowledge, experience, and confidence in their journey and hope to pass on some of their wisdom to your family.

The first spouse decided to return home during a deployment:

> Both my in-laws and my parents welcomed us in during a lengthy deployment, and for longer training periods. My husband and I decided that for my emotional well-being, moving back in with family during the deployment would be best. It's not for everyone. But we are a very close family, and we set up healthy boundaries for our time back in their house. I made sure I did chores, and I handled all the baby night shifts on my own. I respected their home, but they also stepped in and helped plan fun things to pass the time.
>
> They delighted in their granddaughter, and while her daddy could not be around her first year, she was no less loved. She was treasured by so many careful hands, and so was I. It made all the difference in the world to me that I had a family to eat dinner with, to converse with, and that I was able to go on daily walks with my mom. The deployment was hard on our family, but it was also this strange blessing where I watched my parents interact more intimately with our child than they would have had my husband not been gone.
>
> I worry sometimes about us having another child, and then putting our firstborn in school. I'll be more locked into an area than I was on the last deployment cycles. But in chats with my mom and mother-in-law, they have told me, "Honey, don't stress. We'll be there."

It is everything for our family to know that we do not get through raising our child and/or deployments alone. I am only as alone as I choose to be while my Marine is gone. I have to be the one that continues to foster community and take care of our family in his absence. For me, this means leaning into the beautiful grandparent relationships we are fortunate to have right now.

The second spouse recalls a more challenging experience:

My experience with raising my daughter while my husband was deployed was hard. My daughter was only seven months old when my husband left. I decided to move back home for the deployment in order to finish my medical assistant degree. It seemed like what was best. Before he left, we had to get the entire house packed into a storage unit using his truck. I remember the house was insane the months prior to the deployment, due to his flight schedule. I packed 90 percent of the house on my own, and we had just unpacked the house less than a year prior! My daughter was in the baby carrier while I shoved all of our belongings (a four-bedroom house) into plastic bins. …

After the chaos of leaving and landing in Maine, I realized I wasn't going to see my husband for an entire year. But more importantly, our daughter was not going to see her father for an entire year. He missed her first Halloween, first Thanksgiving, first Christmas, first birthday, first steps, first Easter, first words. He missed everything. That was the biggest hurdle we have faced so far. It was not easy … I lived alone, dead set to make it on my own, despite my parents being down the road. Looking back, I was being way too hard-headed.

I remember the most difficult part being that I wasn't able to share our daughter's big moments with her daddy. He was on a ship that did not have any service unless they were in port. We had some serious marital issues come up during that time frame as well. So while I wanted to share our child's exciting moments with him, I also felt resistance toward connecting with him again. It was by far the darkest year of our lives. But we came out of that dark tunnel. My Marine came home, and our daughter spent time with him as if nothing had ever happened.

During that time, my parents provided the best source of support I could ever ask for. With them there to love her so immensely, I survived that deployment. My parents have an undying and unwavering love for my beautiful girl. When I was back in Maine, they came for visits and to hold her so I could get a break. They would spoil her with new books and toys. (They still do!) When I moved back to Hawaii, they were always on video chat with me. It didn't matter if it was a good day or a bad day. They simply wanted to know what was happening in my life and how our child was doing. The other biggest thing that helped was that my parents generously bought our child new clothes. Cute clothes! I'm talking clothes that our daughter would walk into the grocery store and twirl for everyone to see. It may seem silly, but seeing her so confident … made all the difference in our day.

When Families Stay Put During Deployments

There are many reasons why moving during deployment may not be practical or desirable for a Marine family. For example, a working military spouse may prefer the stability their job provides during a deployment and may look for grandparent assistance in other ways. This working military spouse shared:

> As for me, raising a child while my husband is deployed and even while working up to a deployment is both easy and extremely difficult. It's easy because there is only one parent to make everyday decisions. Getting on the same page can be the hardest thing about parenting.
>
> If you are lucky enough to be stationed in a military-friendly community, coworkers, day-care workers, friends, and family are ready to step up. You just have to be willing to ask for help. The hard part is seeing how difficult it is for my Marine to leave us. He will miss a lot of firsts, from milestones to holidays, and I know it makes him so upset to be away. That hurts me because I hate seeing my life partner upset. I also know it will be that much harder for us to acclimate when he gets back from deployment. It's hard enough reconnecting as a couple. It will be just as hard, if not harder, to realign as parents too.
>
> Lastly, we are lucky to have two sets of retired grandparents who will both come out to visit and support the family during this deployment. In addition to grandparents, a sister is coming out to watch our baby so that, as a working spouse, I can go to an important out-of-state conference. We are lucky to have such a supportive family network.

Every family will have to find what works for them during a deployment. This presents a good time to open up healthy conversations about what everyone needs for support and the role grandparents can play in providing it.

Miscarriage, Infertility, and Mental Health Support

Other challenging situations your Marine might face in or out of the military are miscarriages and infertility. A miscarriage occurring in the middle of active duty or when a spouse is deployed adds additional heartache and stress. It can be difficult to talk about this private situation and grief.

If your child or their spouse experiences a miscarriage, remind them of the many resources on base that can help them process their grief and emotions, free of charge. If the person is sensitive or unwilling to go to therapy or counseling in person, there are resources that can help them make anonymous phone calls to a help line, such as Military OneSource, which offers nonmedical counseling, and is confidential for the service member and spouse.

They may not want to talk at all. They may not even want to see others because it's difficult to process or deal with at the moment. It is not an easy conversation, but you do not need to say much to positively support them. If they reach out, a comforting shoulder is invaluable. A few phrases parents/grandparents and their Marine couples going through these challenges have found helpful:

> *"I'm sorry you are going through this."*
>
> *"I am here to listen anytime you need to talk."*
>
> *"I'm here for you, what can I do to help?"*
>
> *"I don't want to bug you about your treatments/results, but I'm here for you if you need me."*

Even from miles away, parents can support a couple struggling with private health challenges. Sometimes that means treading lightly with their hearts and being available for what they need during a difficult time.

Staying Connected

My husband and I feel very blessed to have nine grandchildren. None have lived near enough to just drop by or share common experiences together without lots of planning and preparation. Being separated is not fun, but we take advantage of every opportunity to connect. The quality of time you spend with children and grand-children is what they will remember! Make the most of it and be creative. A few suggestions to get you started:

- Host a virtual baby shower. This is a great way to connect when the parents-to-be are in a different city or country. A good example of a virtual shower was one held when my friend's son and his expecting wife were stationed in Japan. We were asked to mail packages to their overseas address and to save the date for the party. When the day came, the grandmother-to-be hosted a party at her house. She shipped similar decorations to the young couple with instructions to decorate their room to match hers. When the party began, guests also visited via the internet and enjoyed catching up. When the gifts were opened, we took pictures and recorded everyone's excitement. Later the pictures were added to the baby book. This new child was welcomed into the world in a very special way.

- Have a conversation before the baby arrives about the kind of support you can give after the birth. Start with, "How can I help?" and listen to their answer. The couple may have two or more sets of parents who want to help, so flexibility and patience are also great gifts. If you are not close by, you can offer to pay for housecleaning or yard work, or set up delivery of frozen meals. If this is not their first baby, you could offer to be on call or to come a few days early to care for other grandchildren during the delivery or hospital stay.

- If you can, and when the family is ready, plan to visit them to offer the new parents time alone. When couples are parenting full-time, especially without the advantages of grandparents nearby to share this experience, a weekend without responsibilities can go a long way to recharging their parenting batteries—and their relationship as a couple.

- If the baby is born during a Marine's deployment, grandparents can get a letter from the base or commander to allow special shopping privileges and an extended base access pass for commissary and retail stores while helping the Marine spouse.

- When it's not possible or practical for you to visit in person, be available to talk with and share fun moments with grandchildren of all ages using available technology. Invest in a good webcam for computer video calls or set up talk or video apps on your phone or tablet. Younger grandchildren enjoy playing with toys while a grandparent is talking with them on a video call. Older children enjoy showing off school projects or learning a new skill you share with them on a video call. Many schools offer live streaming of athletic events, concerts, and other school programming. Set up a schedule with links on your calendar.

If you are caring for your grandchildren (at your home or theirs) for an extended period of time while their parents are away, you may also need:

- Your name on the daycare and school list, along with any other identification requirements necessary to pick up the children.

- An updated list of medications, allergies, or special needs for children and pets.

- Phone numbers for key contacts, such as teachers, coaches, counselors, doctors, neighbors, or friends.

- Schedules and directions to activities.

- The children's military ID cards.

- Installation access passes if you need to go on base.

- A medical power of attorney to tend to a sick child, local emergency procedures, and directions to local clinics or hospitals.

Mimi's Tips for Long-Distance Grandparenting

Finally, I offer some fun tips to help you strengthen your grandparent-grandchild relationships.

My Song

Consider creating or choosing a song that you sing whenever you see each other online or in person. You can personalize your song by adding the child's name or making up lyrics to a new or old tune. I did this as my unique way of connecting to my grandchildren. What started out as an infant lullaby turned into a song that we sing together with hand gestures now that they are older.

One reason this gift is so special is that my voice became familiar to them. I began singing our song the day they were born. One grandchild even told his mommy not to sing that song because it was Mimi's song. When I told my husband I created a song, he was mildly amused. When I told him he needed a song too, his response was, "Oh, yeah, right … *not!*" We got creative with a song he could agree to and it has been a favorite of all the grandchildren. Making a connection in a unique and special way is a great start to your long-term relationship.

Virtual Playtime

When our grandchildren lived in Hawaii, we lived in Korea. The only time these toddlers saw us was computer to computer. No way were they going to sit still and have a conversation with us, so we had to get creative. I bought two small sets of toys and books, one set for them and one for me. When we visited virtually, I used my toys to entertain and interact with them. I read my books as they turned the pages of their books. We had drum contests to see who could make the loudest noise (to the dismay of their parents, but the kids loved it). We had treasure hunts as they tried to find the toy that I held in my hand, in their toy box. It was fun to see them squeal with delight when we appeared on the screen to play. I started and ended each virtual visit with the "Mimi song," of course!

When we moved back to Virginia and they did too, we were able to visit each other face to face in our homes. My three-year-old granddaughter noticed the pictures of her family in our house and recognized the toys we played with. At first, she was confused because she knew me as a virtual personality. Her face was filled with amazement at the discovery that I was her grandmother and she gave me an extra big hug. Now many years later, we still have a virtual relationship, but she is well aware of who I am, and we share a special relationship in our hearts!

Special Gifts

When I cannot be there for a special occasion, I mail my grandchild a gift. Before I send it, I set up a virtual visit and present the gift to them while it is still in my house. This lets me see their expression of surprise, and it creates an intimate and meaningful moment to talk to them about the gift. If there is an upcoming event for the special occasion—a birthday party, graduation, scout ceremony, or sports competition—this way of sharing allows me to give my gift without becoming a virtual distraction at their party.

I show them the gift unwrapped, and sometimes I wrap it while we're on the call and let them see me put it in the shipping box with their name on it. I may decorate the box in a special way so they can tell it is for them when it arrives at their house.

The day they receive their package is another shared moment of excitement as they know they are remembered in a special way!

Electronic Photo Frames

When you do get to spend time together in person, capture the memories in photos and videos. Sending grandchildren an electronic photo album of family members, events, and celebrations reminds them they are loved and missed. Share stories on video about growing up with their mom or dad. Use a video app to record activities around your house, or share a video moment within the community where you live. Sharing photos or recordings of special family traditions helps grandchildren learn about and feel a part of their extended family. Consider group video chats that include aunts and uncles and cousins to sing birthday songs or share congratulations together.

The long-term benefit when families get together—virtually or in person—is that they become more familiar with each other. Our Marine family's children are now old enough to spend time with us without their parents. Years of connecting through photos, videos, and virtual chats have helped everyone feel more comfortable and look forward to in-person reunions.

Grandparents as Temporary Caregivers

There are many situations that might lead to grandparents becoming temporary caregivers, especially while a Marine is deployed or away on temporary assignment, or when a Marine or spouse encounters special circumstances. For example:

- A single-parent Marine or both parents in a dual-military couple need to be away from home for deployment, temporary duties, or school.

- A Marine or spouse is pregnant or recently gave birth, and needs help caring for themselves, a newborn, or other children.

- Extra caregivers are helpful for a child with special needs.

- A Marine becomes wounded or ill.

- Job demands or other challenges make it difficult to manage household and childcare responsibilities without extra help.

- The family cannot afford childcare and needs the support of family for a period of time.

Family Care Plans

Ask your Marine about their Family Care Plan—a valuable list of collected personal information and forms that permit other designated people, such as grandparents, to act as temporary caregivers if or when the Marine is unable to assist their spouse or children. These occasions can be sudden, confusing, and stressful. Having a plan in place, with an agreement and commitment of support, will put you on the path to success.

Deployment Connections

If you become a caregiver during your Marine's deployment, it is important to find creative ways to help your grandchild stay connected with their parent. You'll want to encourage and help each grandchild to find ways they are comfortable and excited to share special moments throughout the deployment. Letters, care packages, and virtual calls may all be part of the plan. There are many resources and ideas offered through your Marine's family readiness program, and several military-friendly nonprofits also offer organized programs to help.

For example, your Marine can sign up to read a book aloud on the United Through Reading (UTR) app. UTR then sends the video of the parent reading and the physical book to the child. Using a free service like this allows you to help your grandchild feel connected (by watching the video and "reading" their book with their parent) even when your Marine has limited real-time communication options available.

Military Family Books

Books make special gifts at any time for everyone in your Marine's family, but they are especially helpful if you are caring for your grandchildren. Reading stories together can give your grandchild a way to ask you questions, express their feelings, and feel understood.

Being a military kid is tough. They experience all the same challenges and celebrations as kids who aren't in a military family, but they must also learn how to navigate the unique challenges of military life.

Especially be aware if you are caregiving away from their home military base. In a civilian neighborhood or school, other children might not understand what it's like to be a military kid. They may or may not have similar experiences like attending a new school, moving to a new community, being the new kid trying to make new friends, or missing a parent that is away from home for work for long periods of time. Other kids may not have the same fears about a parent's safety.

Reading stories of other kids with similar life experiences can help children of all ages feel less alone. Many books about military life are available online or at bookstores. Military Family Books (MilitaryFamilyBooks.com) is a great place to start for a collection of good books from several publishers. The program is operated by military family members and proceeds help support military family community programs.

Chapter Five

What If? What Next?

LIFE AS A MARINE PARENT IS FULL OF UNKNOWNS. Proper planning can reduce the impact of a crisis. Accidents, illness, and death are part of life in and out of the military experience. Create a plan, including a list of emergency phone numbers, and know where to turn for support.

The Unit, Personal, and Family Readiness Program (UPFRP) officer assigned to your Marine's unit can be one great source of information. The American Red Cross, Military OneSource, and many other resources are also useful to know about, depending on the issue you or your Marine are experiencing.

What if there is a serious illness, accident, or death in your Marine's immediate family?

The American Red Cross is an official agency that offers free communication services in the event of an emergency. If a family member has an emergency, and you must get news to your Marine or they need to return home, the Red Cross is your best resource to communicate with them. Knowing your Marine's rank, military unit, or official mailing address will make it easier and faster for the Red Cross to locate your Marine.

The Red Cross does not authorize emergency leave for service members. Their role is to verify the emergency so the service member's commander can make an educated decision regarding emergency leave, transportation, and need for financial assistance. The Red Cross also facilitates and expedites emergency financial assistance on behalf of military aid societies that determine if a grant or a loan may be offered.

What if your Marine is having serious financial difficulties?

The Navy-Marine Corps Relief Society (a military aid society that works with the Red Cross during a crisis), partners with the Navy and Marine Corps to provide financial, educational, and other assistance to Marines and their families. Eligible service members and their dependents receive free budget counseling and qualify for quick assist, no interest, or low interest loans.

What if your Marine has a serious accident or illness that requires long-term assistance and care?

The Semper Fi Fund provides financial assistance and programming for service members and their families during the hospitalization and recovery of service members who are wounded in combat, critically ill, or catastrophically injured. They offer caregiver support and retreats, assistance with housing and transportation, canine and equestrian programs, camps for kids, adaptive equipment, and more.

Families of patients receiving medical care at major military and VA medical centers may be able to stay for free in a nearby Fisher House. These apartment-style buildings offer private living suites with shared common areas, usually within walking distance of the treatment facility.

What if your Marine or their family needs additional resources to help support their military lifestyle?

Military OneSource offers military families resources and information for all aspects of military life. In addition to its extensive digital library (MilitaryOneSource.mil), this Department of Defense program offers free, confidential, nonmedical counseling in person or by phone from anywhere in the world.

What if your Marine is unable to care for a family member, or a spouse cannot care for themselves or a child?

Family Care Plans make many "what-if" scenarios go more smoothly. In an emergency when a Marine needs short-term support for their family in their absence, this plan enables another designated person to take responsibility for caring for their family. The information contained in a Family Care Plan ensures the person who needs lifestyle support—a dependent family member, single Marine, or dual-military couple—is cared for in a timely manner.

What if your Marine experiences serious work-related difficulties or mental health challenges?

If your Marine experiences sexual harassment or assault; domestic abuse; discrimination based on race, religion, sexual orientation, or other protected status; depression; financial difficulties; suicidal feelings; or similar serious challenges, resources are available on a personal and professional basis as well as through appropriate legal channels. Seeking support, counseling, and advocacy is a sign of courage, and will strengthen the Marine as well as the Marine Corps. As a parent, you can support by being available to listen and by encouraging your Marine to seek out a trusted sponsor who is able to advocate for them and guide them toward the best military support resources for their situation.

The Marine Corps has established official processes and policies to ensure all Marines are treated with dignity and respect. Special training throughout a Marine's career sets a standard for conduct, emphasizing the value of all Marines, reinforcing models of mutual respect, and honoring diversity within the Corps. Several legal, survivor, and investigative resources are available to support Marines and tighten accountability.

Defense Advisory Committee on Women in the Service

The Defense Advisory Committee on Women in the Service (DACOWITS) offers best practices, research, and recommendations in support of women in military service. Their work includes providing the Secretary of Defense recommendations on policies relating to recruitment and retention, employment, integration, well-being, and treatment of professional servicewomen.

Sexual Trauma and Assault

The Marine Corps has a zero-tolerance policy; sexual assault is a direct and flagrant violation of Corps values and principles. The Sexual Assault Prevention and Response program (SAPR) is committed to preventing and eliminating sexual assault in the Corps and providing exceptional care to survivors.

Survivors and those who intervene on their behalf can report an incident of sexual assault without retaliation. Survivors receive confidential 24/7 crisis intervention and referral to support services by credentialed advocates, including medical care and legal representation. The appropriate investigative agency will conduct sensitive independent investigations of reported sexual assault incidents, with a goal to hold offenders accountable.

Programs are in place to stop sexual assault before it occurs and increase reporting of assault incidents. Training programs emphasize how bystander intervention can prevent sexual assault and address acts of retaliation within the Corps.

When a sexual assault is reported, a sexual assault response coordinator (SARC) is assigned to advocate for the survivor and communicate with commanders and unit leaders. SARCs also train other advocates and educate Marines about sexual assault.

Christina Chavez was appointed the first civilian Marine Forces SARC in 2014. She collaborated with the Navy SAPR office to promote inventive ways to educate Marines about sexual assault. Her 2011 Project Unbreakable used photography to give voice to survivors. Her efforts prompted conversations and new ideas for how to encourage and empathize with survivors.

Sexual harassment behavior should always be reported. Unchecked sexual harassment can lead to sexual assault. Immediate and confidential help is available 24/7 through a national or local installation helpline found on the unit or installation website.

Suicide Prevention

Deaths by suicide are preventable. Every suicidal ideation and every suicide attempt must be taken seriously. Prevention requires coordination and collaboration among Marines, their families, and the entire extended Marine Corps community.

Self-injury and voicing thoughts of suicide are signs of distress. For that individual, the pain seems overwhelming and permanent; however, with time and support, service members can overcome this pain. Preventing a death starts with recognizing common risk factors and triggers.

Marines at risk are often going through a personal crisis. This may be legal difficulty, disciplinary action, loss of someone close to them, financial problems, or emotional trauma related to their service. They may talk about feeling trapped, as though no solution or way out of a situation exists. Perhaps they are in transition, changing duty stations, or away from their usual support system.

The Marine Corps DSTRESS Line is a free, anonymous phone and chat service that operates 24/7/365 with Marine-to-Marine counseling, crisis intervention, and referrals.

Conquering Stress with Strength is a workshop where Marine families practice skills for identifying and responding to risks of suicide. They can contact a Family Team Building or Community Counseling Program (CCP) representative to participate.

Research shows that the risk for a repeat suicide-related event or death by suicide is highest during the first ninety days after a suicide attempt or ideation. In the Marine Intercept Program, licensed CCP counselors follow up with Marines throughout those ninety days to provide risk assessment and care coordination.

Family Support for Stressful and Difficult Situations

Families Overcoming Under Stress (FOCUS) is a psychological health program for Marines and their families who are affected by separation, depression, physical injury or disability, loss, trauma, and other life transitions. Clinicians facilitate couples and family counseling sessions and offer skill-building workshops.

During trying times, the stress a Marine feels can be overwhelming, regardless of their job or mission. A Marine may think they are coping in a healthy way, but dealing with everything alone can have unintended consequences for themselves and those around them. Military and family life counselors (MFLCs) are licensed mental health professionals who support service members and their families with non-medical counseling.

Young children are especially aware of the subtle clues parents exhibit when upset, and they may act out with regressive or aggressive behavior. MFLCs conduct special programs for children, youth, and teens, and in K-12 school settings.

I found it helpful to rely on the confidential support of the local chaplains and MFLC counselors. As a commander's spouse for many years, living at numerous bases, I found it reassuring to know they were safe places to voice concerns about relationships within my personal family and relationships throughout our Marine Corps community. When my husband was not around for daily reflection and prayer time, the counselors filled a void. Confidentiality was the key, and no topic was too personal to share. This support kept me strong through those dark times when I needed spiritual or psychological advice to keep my faith and spirits alive.

Knowing these resources are available can reassure hometown families that their loved ones have the support they need. Keep an open perspective on any life circumstance, and know there are many resources available for your Marine!

What if your Marine faces civil situations regarding loans, leases, or major purchases? What are their rights?

Your Marine has protections that provide a sense of financial security at different times in their lives, outside their duties, training, and combat scenarios. The Servicemembers Civil Relief Act (SCRA) offers protections for service members and their families in many different areas, from mortgages to life insurance. Your Marine can get free advice through Military OneSource on how the SCRA applies to their individual circumstances.

Some SCRA protections include reduced interest rates, postponement of foreclosures, deferred income taxes, eviction prevention, postponed civil court matters, protection for small-business owners, termination of lease agreements, prevention of repossession of property, life insurance coverage protection, voting rights in your Marine's home state, and more.

What if your Marine and their spouse separate?

Moving forward with a divorce can be the most difficult, costly, and emotional decision a military couple makes. It might also be the proper and necessary path to the start of a new life. As parents, you can offer your willingness to listen even if other support options are limited due to distance, personalities, or privacy.

Couples can use Military OneSource as an information source or to set up meetings with a counselor, spiritual advisor, wellness coach, or financial or legal counselor, or to find support for other family members. In-person and virtual opportunities to connect with professional advocates during this challenging time can help your Marine focus on self-care, hone communication skills to heal relationships, or process their feelings as they work through this transition and strive to remain mission-ready.

As a couple goes through the process of weighing options through counseling or legally separating, they both need to tend to their own emotional wellness. Even if they feel confident in their decision and ready to move forward, they might decide to ask for extra help. Child and youth behavioral counselors are available to help children process how the divorce is affecting them. Encourage your Marine to take advantage of military resources.

This transition may also be difficult for you as a parent. It is natural to feel protective when your child is hurting, no matter their age. In a separation or divorce, extended family members are impacted as well. You can be loyal and supportive without being for or against any individual. Relationships and situations are more complex than they appear. Listen, guide your loved ones toward professional support systems, and attend to your own self-care.

Legal Considerations of Divorce

While state law and local procedures largely govern divorce, certain federal statutes and military regulations may be applicable to your Marine's situation. For instance, the Servicemembers Civil Relief Act helps protect service members' legal rights when called to active duty.

Service members and their families have access to legal advice at no cost through installation legal assistance offices. Military lawyers, called judge advocates (JAGs), are available to help your Marine understand the legal implications of their divorce. The JAG officer will talk with either the Marine or the spouse, to avoid a potential conflict of interest. They cannot represent either one in family court but can refer them to a civilian lawyer.

Resiliency

As your Marine and their family live the daily routines of military life, they build a special set of skills from their own experiences and from those of others around them. The stories in this book are reminders that strength comes from sharing new experiences with others in the "same boat." Moving around, exploring new places, and stepping out of one's comfort zone develop new characteristics and personality traits.

Marine families see firsthand the "what-if and what-next" scenarios that play out all around them. By relying on each other for support, they learn from their similar experiences. Being armed with knowledge, training, and good resources is the best way to be prepared for anything, the readiness attitude that is expected in many facets of Marine life. The lifestyle of the Corps comes with risks, challenges, and problems. The qualities of resiliency go a long way if and when the "what-ifs" happen.

As a Marine parent, your resiliency will strengthen as well. Joining in conversations in parent support groups and engaging with parents of other Marines in their unit can help you feel connected to your Marine's lifestyle and provide ideas for you to take care of your own "what-if" situations.

Chapter Six

Fears Realized

OUR MARINE IS STILL OUR CHILD IN MY HEART. Nothing compares to the empty feeling I have on occasions when I know he might be suffering from illness, trauma, or injury caused by his Marine Corps experience. In the unfortunate event that your Marine is wounded, ill, or injured, know there is help and hope.

An appointed casualty assistance command representative (CACR) in your Marine's unit is available twenty-four hours a day, seven days a week. They will answer your questions on the casualty assistance process and provide comprehensive support to next of kin throughout recovery and transition.

Wounded, Ill, Injured

Early in the Iraq conflict, when many Marines were returning home with significant wounds of war, one wounded warrior commander said he wanted to recover with his Marines. Soon after, special units were created to respond to the types of care and recovery that allowed Marines to stay together while they healed. The success of this kind of care was attributed to the support that only a Marine could give to another.

Wounded Warrior Regiment (WWR)

The Wounded Warrior Regiment supports Marines who are wounded, ill, or injured, and supports their families, whether or not the injury was incurred in combat, and whether the Marines are assigned to the regiment, remain with their parent unit, or have already transitioned to civilian life. The WWR motto is _Etiam in pugna_ or "Still in the fight." Marines stay with their units as long as the unit can adequately support their medical and recovery needs. Marines with the most complicated needs are assigned to one of the WWR elements. WWR resources and experts are also available to recovering Marines, families, and command leadership through regiment call centers and battalion contact centers. Battalions work closely with your Marine and medical staff to help determine the most appropriate resources for medical and psychological issues. Programs assist caregivers and family members in managing the recovery and transition of your wounded, ill, or injured Marine.

Services are available to active duty, reserve, and veteran Marines and their families. The regimental headquarters in Quantico, Virginia, command the operation of two Wounded Warrior battalions (WWBn) and multiple detachments in locations around the globe, including major military treatment facilities and rehabilitation centers. Each WWBn also has a contact center with representatives who monitor a Marine's recovery and provide information on programs and resources.

Marine assignments to the WWR come through casualty reports, a medical officer's recommendation, or a unit commander's recommendation. Marines who qualify for recovery care coordinator (RCC) assistance receive a comprehensive recovery plan; a Marine's daily activities are based on the identified steps to reach the goals in the recovery plan.

Recovery, Rehabilitation, and Reintegration Process

The goal of the recovery process is to attain quality of life and financial stability, reinforced by mental, moral, and physical strength. WWR staff provide medical advocacy and administrative support and assist recovering Marines through four specific lines of operation (LOO): mind, body, spirit, and family.

Mind LOO focuses on sharpness of the mind, concentration,

memory, understanding, and increased ability to learn and com-
prehend, using college courses, vocational training, on-the-job
training, internships, and professional military education.

Body LOO creates a foundation for health and physical fitness,
using medical and physical therapy, diet and nutrition education,
and competitions in the Warrior Athlete Reconditioning Program.

Spirit LOO encourages life balance and control, positive relationships, a sense of purpose and meaning, acceptance and growth
with life challenges, and connection with a greater power, using
religious programs, behavioral services, and extension outreach.

Family LOO promotes open communication, well-being, resiliency, shared responsibilities, redefined roles, and a safe and
appreciative environment, using religious programs, behavioral
services, and family readiness programs.

Medical Discharge

Getting out of the military on medical discharge is challenging, and is never "Plan A" for the Marine or their family. Medical discharge can be due to severe injuries sustained in combat,
in training, or an illness that prevents them from being able to
continue to serve.

Regardless of the circumstances, it can result in a sense of fail-
ure or frustration, and perhaps also a sense of relief. A medical
discharge is usually a long process and a test in patience, involving
multiple medical tests, rehab clinics, therapies, and evaluations.
The process can be discouraging for even the most positive person
and make it harder for your Marine to relate to their fellow service
members and families. During this process, support from friends
and family is crucial. Knowing that they are not alone and have
people who care about them can make a monumental difference
in how your Marine comes out of the experience.

One positive aspect of the process is the option to be involved
in the discharge experience in advance—a rarity in active service.
This gives your Marine time to plan their next steps and think
about the life they want to carve out in the civilian sector. Two

Marine families shared their stories to illustrate how being medically discharged impacted their future.

The first Marine spouse shared:

> Life was very difficult for our family when my husband's headaches and migraines started. We experienced a lack of continuity of care, made even more challenging between multiple deployments and moves. However, once we moved to Hawaii, and my Marine had the opportunity to have good continuity of care for more than six months, things started to get better for him, his health, and our family.
>
> We thought we might be in the clear until we were hit with the stress of the medical board. My husband wanted so badly to be a career Marine and had been designated to be one, as long as he made the promotion list. He was devastated that the headaches and migraines were going to affect his career in such a negative way. Yet as he continued through the medical board process, he was able to recognize that these invisible injuries would always be part of his life. He understood that leading Marines in combat was not going to be a good fit for him, especially with other Marine lives at stake.
>
> The medical board took one and a half years to complete, and in that time, he learned that he had a traumatic brain injury (TBI) from his tour in Iraq. The TBI was the cause of his frequent and debilitating migraines. He also learned how to properly medicate himself so that it would not affect his daily routine with his family. The results from the medical board led him to be medically retired. He ended up rating 100 percent disability through the VA. It was honestly very hard for him to accept.
>
> During the transition, he worked to network and sought employment outside the Marine Corps.

Transitioning from our duty station of Hawaii out into the civilian world had its own set of unanticipated challenges. Our time difference with most of the US mainland was anywhere from three to six hours behind. The majority of companies were not willing to do an in-person interview because of the cost of travel to fly him off the island. Thankfully, one company on the West Coast was very interested in hiring my husband and willing to fly him out to San Diego for an interview.

That family was able to secure employment in San Diego and made a life-changing move to the civilian sector. They purchased a home and had another child. While it was hard to leave Marine Corps life behind, their transition was a positive one.

The second family's Marine was medically discharged for progressive back pain, as he was unable to pass standard physical fitness tests and deemed unfit for duty. He also received full disability. They decided to use the GI Bill, and the Marine went back to school for his master's degree. When deciding where to complete his program, the family sought a location closer to their extended family. His spouse secured a job with her family's business, and he found work at the university. He condensed his time away from home by taking courses and working on campus. Before getting out, they sold many of their belongings to fellow military families and downsized tremendously. They enjoyed being closer to family, but it was still a big change being away from their military community and adjusting to housing and financial changes.

The medical board process gives most families time to research their benefits. In addition to the standard benefits given to all service members, disabled veterans are eligible to receive additional coverage from the VA, including disability compensation and medical coverage for the service-related injury. Added funding is available for vocational rehabilitation, readjustment counseling, career education, ADA (Americans with Disabilities Act) home modifications, and many others.

The transition from a full active-duty service life to the civilian sector is an adjustment, whether the Marine is medically discharged or chooses on their own to leave service.

The Long Road to Recovery

The following is one mother's story of her wounded Marine, adapted with permission from Semper Fi Fund. The story is a testament to the care and support this family received after their Marine was wounded in combat. The scenario is not uncommon, since thousands of parents have assisted and supported their Marine as caregivers.

Robin Carpenter received the kind of phone call every mother dreads.

> "We got home from church at noon and there was a message from Quantico to call back with regards to Lance Corporal Kyle Carpenter. We knew right then. They told us on that initial phone call that he was the worst-case injured. I just wanted to be with him, I couldn't bear that he was by himself."
>
> While serving in Afghanistan, the twenty-one-year-old infantryman had thrown himself in front of a grenade to protect a fellow Marine. His body was riddled with shrapnel and he suffered what the South Carolina legislature later called "catastrophic wounds in the cause of freedom."
>
> He suffered severe injuries to his face, including the loss of his right eye and most of his teeth. His jaw and right arm were shattered.
>
> When Kyle was being transported back to the States after his injury, he traveled with another injured service member, an Army sniper named Ryan. Robin was unable to be with her son, but Ryan's mother was on the plane.
>
> "She spent time holding Ryan's hand and Kyle's hand," Robin says, "and she told me … Kyle was

moaning, 'Mom' all the way back from Germany."

It was while Kyle was recovering from his injuries in Bethesda, Maryland, that Robin first encountered the Semper Fi Fund.

"What they've done for us—the services, emotional support, unconditional love—there's not enough words for me to describe. They truly do treat these combat-wounded service members as if they were their own children. … It's kind of like they know a need before you even know you need a need."

Kyle underwent dozens of surgeries on the road to recovery. He became the youngest living recipient of the Medal of Honor. A few years after being injured, he ran the Marine Corps Marathon!

When asked if her experiences have taught her any lessons that would apply to all mothers, not just military moms, Robin referred to a favorite saying: *You never know how strong you are until strong is the only choice you have.*

"People say to me all the time, 'I don't know how you do this.' Kyle's had about thirty to forty surgeries, and I've sat in a waiting room hour after hour. … You do what you have to do," Robin says.

"I believe God gave me the strength to get up and put one foot in front of the other, and that it was my mission to get him well and to get him independent again. … We just push through it every day."

"I just have so much respect for any parent—if you have raised children, you have done something. It's hard work. There's nothing more precious and nothing more valuable. I cannot imagine not being a mom, but you have to be tough."

The Carpenters and my family have a wonderful friendship that began at events surrounding Kyle's award ceremony. Since

Robin and I are both South Carolina girls, the opportunities to visit each other have been fun. I've seen her strength firsthand.

At a Marine Corps Marathon, I stood beside Robin while she tracked Kyle's progress along the race course through his location chip. This race was especially challenging because the weather was warmer that day, which increased the runners' dehydration and exhaustion. Robin knew Kyle wanted to beat his last personal best time, hoping the previous few years had given his body a chance to heal more and be at optimal strength. It looked like he was on the way to achieving this goal. Our spirits were high. Then word came that he was taken to an aid station along the way around mile twenty, six miles shy of the finish. This news would concern anyone supporting their runner, but it was especially concerning for Robin, given Kyle's history of combat-related injuries. Time dragged on as she waited for updates on his condition.

Robin knew the physical and psychological strength it takes to finish a marathon under the best of conditions, and her son was facing even greater challenges. Robin's concern was as much for Kyle's emotional well-being and the disappointment he would feel for not having achieved his time goal.

Kyle lost about two hours, so he did not achieve a personal best record, but he did get his medal. He signed a waiver for the medical officials to let him finish the race.

Robin and I agree that this was a more perfect end to the story. Yes, beating his previous time would have been a great accomplishment, but returning to the race and beating the odds that said he would not finish, is a great testament to his character. What an example he and his mom set, to never give up.

Robin and I enjoy a special relationship, Marine mom to Marine mom. I highly recommend building relationships with other Marine parents. No matter your experiences, you will likely find much in common through your connection to the Corps. And those friendships will provide support in many ways over the years.

Post-Traumatic Stress

Kyle's visible wounds healed through surgeries and physical rehabilitation. He proved that recovery to a full and active life is possible. The hidden wounds of trauma and tragedy are more difficult to detect. Warriors and veterans carry memories of war, accidents, sexual or physical attack, or other traumatic events that leave emotional wounds and scars.

The National Center for PTSD (ptsd.va.gov) provides support and information about post-traumatic stress (PTS). While each person experiences PTS in their own way, common warning signs and symptoms include:

- *Reliving the traumatic event.* A reminder of the trauma, such as hearing fireworks or gunfire sounds, or seeing a news report about the type of disaster your Marine lived through, can trigger very real and frightening memories or nightmares, feeling as if the event is happening again.

- *Avoiding reminders of the event.* Certain people or situations may create painful reminders of the trauma, so a person with PTS tries to avoid them. For example, someone who was assaulted might avoid places similar to the assault site. A combat veteran might avoid crowds if it feels dangerous to be around a lot of people.

- *Having more negative thoughts and feelings.* Negative feelings, sadness, loss of interest in things enjoyed before the trauma, and numbness are common, as is a new sense that the world is not safe, or they can't trust people and must be on guard. Guilt and shame for the event itself can occur. Positive emotions may be hard to express.

- *Feeling on edge.* Feeling jittery or experiencing hyperarousal makes it hard to relax and can cause trouble sleeping and concentrating. Sudden anger and irritability are common. Unhealthy behaviors may include smoking, abusing drugs and alcohol, driving aggressively, or engaging in high-risk activities.

Proper diagnosis and treatment for PTS can lessen intensity of symptoms and result in a better quality of life. Untreated PTS usually does not get better on its own; symptoms don't just go away over time. Even if your Marine feels like they can handle their symptoms now, they may get worse, especially if symptoms have lingered for more than a year without professional treatment.

Not all Marines experience post-traumatic stress. Distress in life due to financial, relationship, or health issues, and any traumatic death are common to the general population. Your Marine may just be stressed or extremely anxious over life events because they are struggling to find answers or a pathway to solutions.

You may feel reluctant to get involved. If you express your concern, your Marine may say, "You don't understand because you have not been there." Talk to them with compassion, encouragement, and love. Your Marine has faced many difficult situations where they have been held to a significant standard of accountability. They can handle the scrutiny. And you know your Marine, so trust your instincts.

This is a time to help your Marine strengthen their resolve to get help, like strengthening a muscle. It will get stronger when they exercise it, by talking about it. Gather multiple resources and agents who can engage with the kind of care and concern you want for your Marine. You may have crossed this bridge of difficult or reluctant conversations when they were in their teen years. Don't give them a pass not to talk. Doing so sends them further down the road to isolation and further distress.

Another resource you can tune into is an online radio program, *All Marine Radio*. Founder and host, Mike McNamara, is a veteran Marine and no stranger to trauma. He has interviewed Corps leadership and Marines of all ranks on his broadcasts and podcasts, offering a variety of perspectives on dealing with traumatic events and other stressful moments. Their experiences range from Vietnam to Desert Storm, Iraq, and Afghanistan. Mac refers to "Blunt Force Truths" to describe the approach Marines have with each other to confront problems that need to be addressed.

Your Marine is not alone, and neither are you. Separately or together, you can discover a pathway to healing.

Death of a Marine

I cannot begin to know or describe the feeling of losing a Marine. I pray you will never experience it firsthand.

Death is an unthinkable but very real possibility given the high risks of the job. Even if your Marine is not in a war zone or hazardous environment, their daily training routines and exercises with live fire can still put them in harm's way. The most important factor for the parents and family of a Marine to know is that you are not alone. When a death occurs, a community of love and support comes together. Marines mourn, grieve, and honor their own.

In the event of a Marine's death, or if a Marine becomes missing in action, great care is taken to deliver the sad news. A casualty assistance calls officer (CACO) along with a chaplain will appear in person, in uniform, at the door of the next of kin designated by the Marine. CACOs assist with further information, burial arrangements, applications for benefits and entitlements, obtaining investigation reports, and other pertinent issues.

Department of Defense's Death Gratuity Program

The DoD's death gratuity program provides a special tax-free payment to eligible survivors of service members who die while on active duty or while serving in certain reserve statuses. The death gratuity is the same regardless of the cause of death and is intended to assist survivors with their financial needs during the period immediately following the death and before other survivor benefits are available.

A Marine may designate any person or persons to receive up to 100 percent of the death gratuity (in 10 percent increments), with any remaining undesignated amount payable according to a prescribed hierarchy, such as spouse, children, parents, and other next of kin. Members may designate eligible survivors, at any time, by updating their DD Form 93, Record of Emergency Data.

Gold Star Families

Parents of every generation have mourned the loss of their children killed while defending their country. American Gold Star Mothers, Inc. was created by a group of mothers in 1928 to honor the loss and sacrifice of those families. The national organization is named after the gold star stitched on a flag that families hang in their windows in honor of the deceased veteran.

A Gold Star family is the immediate family member(s) of a fallen service member who died while serving in a time of conflict. (A Blue Star family is the immediate family of a living service member during a time of conflict. The family may hang a Blue Star Service Flag, with one blue star for each service member.)

President Woodrow Wilson coined the term Gold Star mother after authorizing a request from the Women's Committee of the Council of National Defenses in 1918. Mothers who had lost a child who served in a war could wear a gold star on their black arm band. This led to the tradition of a gold star covering a blue star on the service flag to show that the service member had passed.

A Gold Star Service Flag can be hung in the window by a family member to honor their fallen service member. The number of gold stars indicates the number of people who died. Family members authorized to display the flag include spouses, parents, children, siblings, stepparents, stepchildren, stepsiblings, half-siblings, adopted parents, adopted children, and adopted siblings of a US service member. The flag can also be displayed by an organization to honor its members who served and died during conflict.

After the passage of a joint congressional resolution in 1936, the last Sunday of September was recognized as Gold Star Mothers' Day. President Barack Obama amended it in 2011 to include the recognition of all Gold Star family members on this day. The DoD also issues Gold Star lapel pins to spouses, parents, and children of service members killed in the line of duty.

You can honor surviving family members by recognizing the significance of service flags and lapel pins. Also keep in mind that the Marine Corps is a close community. When one family is impacted, all are impacted. Fellow Marines may not be labeled Gold Star families because they are not technically related to the fallen, but they feel the loss of a fellow warrior as though they've lost a sibling. They may not display a gold star on a flag or a pin, but that gold star is etched on their heart, and will remain there for the rest of their lives.

Honoring Your Fallen Marine

There are many ways to honor a fallen Marine and continue their legacy. Some families choose to turn their grief into service to others. Some find creative ways to preserve their story. Some gather together with others who have been through similar circumstances. Each person's grief is unique, and each Marine's life is a special one to celebrate.

Socks for Heroes—LCpl. Donald Hogan, USMC

After the death of their son, Jim and Carla Hogan began a drive called "Socks for Heroes" to continue their support for Marines. They sought out the Marines their son had served with, at first to understand what had happened, then to find a meaningful way to support them. It turns out what they needed was socks. On the front lines, they did not have laundry facilities; a simple change of socks was a luxury.

Jim and Carla initially solicited sock donations from other sources, but as the squad's redeployment neared, Jim personally purchased 230 pairs, three pairs per Marine. Word got out, and soon they had requests from other servicemembers, as well as donations from local businesses to support their new project.

Since 2011, the Hogans have shipped more than 800,000 pairs of socks to deployed servicemembers! Carla also became involved in American Gold Star Mothers.

I met Carla at the memorial service for her son, held at Camp Pendleton. And I saw her again and again as she returned to honor more Marines from her son's unit who were killed in operations in Afghanistan. Although she did not seek attention, her presence was clearly recognized by the Marines who served with her son.

Carla is still active in her community and now holds competitive shooting fundraisers. She says working in remembrance of her son allows her to never forget him. She says, "This will never fill the void his death left in my life," but that turning her attention to others is the best way forward for her.

Brothers Forever—1st Lt. Travis Manion, USMC, and
Lt. Brendan Looney, USN

Colonel Tom Manion, USMC (Ret) and journalist Tom Sileo coauthored the book *Brothers Forever* to share the story of Tom's son, Marine Travis Manion, and his brother-in-arms, Navy SEAL Brendan Looney.

Tom also travels the country conducting leadership programs to inspire young people to live with character and to serve others. Runners who enter races to support the Travis Manion Foundation are inspired by Travis's words, *"If not me, then who?"*—the words Travis spoke in response to his willingness to deploy for a second time, the deployment he did not survive. Those words were taken up as the mantra for the foundation. Many support their cause, literally and figuratively, finishing the races to honor Travis and Brendan.

Heart of a Marine Foundation—LCpl. Phillip Frank, USMC

I met Georgette and Roy Frank at an event I attended with my husband. I noticed Georgette's lapel pin, shaped like a heart, and asked her what it meant. She shared the story of the loss of their son. Inspired by the way Phil lived his twenty years, the Franks created the Heart of a Marine Foundation in honor of his service. Through their fundraising, they purchase medical devices to assist wounded, ill, and injured Marines in their recovery. They credit the experience with saving them from their own grief.

Georgette and I exchanged pins that evening. I gave her my small lapel pin of an eagle, globe, and anchor to express my sympathy for their loss and my gratitude for their service.

Two years later, my husband was recovering from back surgery and rehabilitating at Balboa Naval Hospital for the month to follow. One day, he was given a cane to replace his walker. Immediately I recognized the Heart of a Marine logo on the cane. A tear for Phil and his dear parents filled my eyes, and a prayer of gratitude filled my heart. Along with many others they have supported, we are so thankful they chose to turn their sorrow into service.

The Sugar Bear Foundation—LtCol. Mario Carazo, USMC

Lieutenant Colonel Mario Carazo, call sign Sugar Bear, was a Cobra pilot shot down in Afghanistan. His wife Jennifer created The Sugar Bear Foundation to support surviving spouses and children of the fallen. The foundation carries on his legacy of caring for those in his command and their families. The foundation's forum assists spouses facing transitions and provides social and financial support in partnership with the Marine Corps Recruit Depot (San Diego) Command Museum.

Marine Corps Marathon—Fallen Heroes

Each year, Marines and other runners participate in the Marine Corps Marathon, a 26.2-mile race in Washington, DC, and Arlington, Virginia. The course wraps around meaningful landmarks and monuments, finishing uphill at the Marine Corps War Memorial.

Any marathon is a grueling test of a runner's physical and mental toughness. The last leg is especially difficult, requiring a runner to focus on why it's important for them to finish. While participants run for a variety of reasons—competition, bucket list, or simply the challenge—many Marine Corps Marathon runners race in honor of a fallen servicemember. Individuals and memorial teams often wear their heroes' names on their shirts as a public display of their motivation.

If you are physically able to put in the hard work of training, this marathon can be a meaningful way to bond with others who are running to preserve and honor a loved one's memory. If you are not able to run the marathon yourself, your encouraging cheers from the sidelines may be just what someone else needs.

Taking Care of Yourself

I cannot stress enough the importance of seeking support for yourself after you experience a trauma, tragedy, natural disaster, or death. We parents, caregivers, and survivors are strong in our own way, but we can be strengthened by the support of others. Many organizations have outstanding programs. Use them. Read books in the quiet of your home. Talk with others.

Tragedy Assistance Program for Survivors (TAPS.org)

Tragedy Assistance Program for Survivors (TAPS) offers adult and youth programs for those grieving the loss of a military loved one. Survivors can gather at seminars, grief camp, retreats, and expeditions. TAPS staff can connect loved ones to counseling in their community and help navigate benefits and resources.

Hope for the Warriors (HopeForTheWarriors.org)

The veterans' service organization Hope for the Warriors helps service members, veterans, and Blue and Gold Star families restore a sense of self, family, and hope. Programs focus on transition, well-being, and connection with each other and the community.

National Resource Directory (NRD.gov)

The National Resource Directory connects wounded warriors, service members, veterans, and their families and caregivers to programs and services that support recovery, rehabilitation, and community reintegration. The website lists vetted resources on a variety of topics.

Hidden Heroes (HiddenHeroes.org)

To inspire community participation and increase resources, the Elizabeth Dole Foundation established a growing network of cities dedicated to sharing best practices and streamlining services for military caregivers.

Chapter Seven

Turning Pride into Purpose

YOUR MARINE'S MILITARY SERVICE IS AN OPPORTUNITY to find new purpose as a parent and community member. The Marine Corps community is a tight-knit group, bonded by the sacrifice and service that marks military life. If Marines visit your town or city, invite your family, friends, and community to see for themselves what this pride is all about. There are many creative ways to support your Marine and their unit, and to participate in local activities to honor Marines.

When Mike and JoAnn became Marine parents, they sent letters to their son at boot camp and added letters with words of encouragement to his squad-mates. They donated to Stand Alone Marines to support new Marine graduates whose families were not able to attend. During their son's many deployments, they mailed frequent care packages to supply their son's fireteam with necessary items and extra treats from home. Mike donated sports memorabilia auction items for military charities through the small business he works for; he framed them himself, and his contributions earned thousands of dollars for worthy causes. Their son transitioned from enlistment to a commissioned lieutenant, and their journey continues to support his platoons and companies.

Mike says their generosity has been motivated by stories their son shares about his brothers and sisters in arms, who sometimes need the kind of support only a parent can offer. JoAnn talks of the pride she has for their son, knowing his journey has been filled with multiple personal and emotional challenges. He chose to focus on his goals and work hard to achieve every success. The whole family works as a team, making a difference for others.

Aside from personally investing time and talent to directly support and encourage individual Marines, you can also give money or volunteer hours to worthy and reputable nonprofit organizations that support Marines. Charity rating services can help you understand how these organizations operate and determine which you want to support.

Join the Marine Corps League

Marine parents may join the Marine Corps League (MCL), an organization founded in 1937 to provide a legacy of support for Marines, veterans, chaplains, and families. MCL has more than six hundred detachments and auxiliaries throughout the US.

MCL members participate in graveside ceremonies and memorials, advocate for veterans in need of medical aid, host local parades and Marine Corps Birthday celebrations, volunteer for Toys for Tots, and more. The MCL Foundation sponsors scholarships and financial assistance to veterans and families. The MCL Auxiliary's Operation Little Angel works with local child abuse centers, children's homes, and other local agencies.

League members are a valuable network for Marines transitioning to civilian life. They have connections to employers and firsthand knowledge about VA benefits and services, and they partner with the Marine for Life Program.

MCL is a huge sponsor and supporter of the Young Marines program, for youth ages eight to eighteen. The program offers youth development opportunities that nurture and develop responsible citizens and promote a healthy lifestyle.

Get Involved in Your Community

Offer support to Marines and military families you meet in your own community to honor their sacrifice and service. Even if you don't live near a military installation, you may find Marines closer to home than you realize. From Alaska to Florida, Maine to California, and all parts in between, you have an opportunity to support Marines. Marines work all over America, many in civilian communities at recruiting offices, Reserve centers, National Guard units, and units supporting special activities. Marines may attend a local college through the Marine Enlisted Commissioning Education Program (MECEP), Naval Reserve Officers' Training Corps (NROTC), or other training facilities as students, or they may work as staff members.

If you don't have an opportunity to directly support Marines in your community, you can visit the websites of local veterans organizations to find and attend events that honor and celebrate veterans, service members, and military families. A few ideas:

- Attend local patriotic celebrations, ceremonies, and memorial services. The Marine Corps League and Auxiliary, Women Marines Association, Veterans of Foreign Wars, and American Legion sponsor and support events that may interest you.

- Volunteer to support Toys for Tots, make Quilts of Valor, or crochet blankets for the Navy-Marine Corps Relief Society for newborn babies.

- Ask local civic or religious groups and veterans organizations to sponsor Marines and their units by sending packages or writing letters to Marines in remote locations. Marines serving as embassy guards and in other foreign duties can feel isolated and will appreciate the encouragement.

- Support national organizations whose mission is to support military service members and their families, for example: United Service Organizations (USO), Armed Forces YMCA, National Military Family Association, Blue Star Families, and United Through Reading.

- Ask your school district's administrators about ways you

can support local Junior Reserve Officers' Training Corps (JROTC) high school programs, which train youth in citizenship and leadership.

• Contribute to the Marine Corps Scholarship Foundation to help fund college tuition for children of fallen Marines and Fleet Marine Force (FMF) Corpsmen.

Getting involved in programs and events that support and celebrate those who serve is about more than volunteering your time to make a difference for others. You may gain a deeper perspective yourself and develop close relationships as you share your Marine parent experiences and turn your pride into purpose!

Mama Jewell

One Marine mom's nickname, Mama Jewell, is a testament to the love and support she shows for Marines in her local community. She keeps an open-door policy for any and all Marines in her small hometown in Maryland. It started with weekend visits when her son came home and brought along other Marines. Her home became the gathering place. When her son deployed, she adopted others who considered them family for holiday celebrations. One Thanksgiving she prepared three separate items: meatloaf, ham, and spaghetti, the favorite dishes of the visiting Marines, to give them a familiar taste of home. When her son got married, Mama Jewell hosted all the Marines from out of town, who slept on couches and any empty floor space. Her new daughter-in-law lived with them through a deployment and a hurricane evacuation, during which she gave birth to her second baby.

Later, Mama's second son was stationed in their hometown as a Marine recruiter, and the hospitality lived on. She took on a new role when she offered support to "Poolies," a nickname given to those waiting to enter boot camp, and their parents. Mama Jewell and her family created a notable reputation of caring for all who know them. The story is not over yet, because their son, the recruiter, recruited his younger brother! Mama Jewell intends to offer a home for all Marines who pass her way, for many more years.

Stories like these are a reminder that opportunities for acts of goodness and kindness are all around. You can play a big part in your own community to help when a dream is unfulfilled, when Marines or their families feel overwhelmed, and especially when trauma enters the picture. Whether it is supporting and encouraging families, celebrating successes, or offering help when tragedy strikes, love of Corps and country lives on when we show appreciation, gratitude, and support for others and their cause.

Read Marine Parent Blogs

If you do an online search for Marine mom or Marine dad blogs, dozens of sites pop up. Their stories revolve around boot camp, deployments, and reunions. Themes center on pride, hopes, and anxieties, and give glimpses into the journey they are traveling. Visiting these sites can be encouraging and eye-opening. Parents speak candidly about the ups and downs of their Marine's life. Sometimes the downs inspire us to want to reach out to offer resources or counseling and support options. You may find negative comments online or in person about military service, but those should not define the impression you have about the Marine Corps. Life is a mix of those who have good news and those who don't. If you choose to reply online, do so with encouragement and positive information.

For the most part, you will find blog posts full of love, humor, and entertaining stories. Ask your Marines for some stories of their own that you can add to your journal as a snapshot of life in the Corps. Starting a blog yourself is a way to contribute and share your experiences too. Keep in mind operational security (OPSEC) and make it entertaining!

Find Your Own Creative Outlets

Turning your time into talent can be cathartic in many ways. I turned to quilting to fill the void of my empty nest. I made quilts for military hospital patients and newborn babies and discovered a creative outlet and enjoyable hobby that gave me an opportunity to focus my energy in a productive way.

What are your interests? You may find your new talent in art, music, nature, or in your community. You and your Marine will both grow in new and exciting ways on this journey.

Chapter Eight

Careers and Transitions

THE LENGTH OF YOUR MARINE'S CAREER is determined by many factors. Marines can decide to leave service once their contract obligations are met. If they desire to continue their service beyond their initial commitment, Marines must remain eligible to serve and must prove they possess the physical ability, technical skills, and professional leadership qualities to be promoted. Their performance in all areas will be continually assessed as your Marine progresses in rank and responsibility.

How fast they can run and how many pull-ups and sit-ups your Marine can do will be measured as a test of strength and endurance. Training requirements like firing rifles and pistols, as well as knowledge of tactical and technical elements, will determine whether your Marine meets the highest levels of proficiency. Uniforms will be meticulously inspected. On- and off-duty behaviors will also be judged by superiors against the highest standards of moral and ethical conduct and against your Marine's peers.

The promotion process varies by rank; proficiency and conduct standards are different for junior and senior enlisted Marines, staff noncommissioned officers, and officers. All Marines must take personal initiative to improve a broad range of skills.

If a Marine is wounded, ill, or injured, and cannot meet physical or technical requirements, they may be offered an opportunity to begin learning a new Military Occupational Specialty (MOS) in an area they are capable of performing. In other circumstances, if they are found guilty of legal, ethical, or moral issues, these can be grounds for earlier than expected dismissal. Staffing or technical needs of the Department of Defense or the Marine Corps also factor into promotion decisions.

In their positive, optimistic, dedicated way, Marines continue to strive daily to meet and exceed the requirements they have control over, rather than dwell on the factors that may end their careers unexpectedly.

Staying safe in all they do and securing their future through good judgment, goal setting, prudent spending and saving, and clean living helps them stay successful and beat the odds. If they have applied these principles during service, then preparing to leave the service will likely be met with the same planning and preparation, attitude, and success.

Professional and Career Development

Once a Marine is first assigned their Military Occupational Specialty (MOS) rating, advancement requirements are clearly and specifically spelled out in an MOS Roadmap guide. Roadmaps are critical, systematic steps taken to ensure a Marine's professional advancement can lead to a fulfilling career and retirement.

The first Marine leadership principle listed is, "Know yourself and seek improvement." Leadership is a lifelong practice for Marines, as is professional and career development. These are carefully planned out in a series of specific trainings, education, and assignments according to the MOS Roadmap. Statistically, career progression is easier to achieve in the lower ranks. As a Marine starts competing for higher-ranking jobs based on exceptional merit, skills, and the needs of the Corps, the Marine Corps must be more selective, and the competition for those jobs is greater. An honorable life of service for your Marine in uniform is possible for twenty, thirty, or even forty years.

Personal Growth and Financial Fitness

Though Marines can rely on the MOS Roadmap for career success, they also must drive their own pursuit of personal fulfillment and excellence. Being a Marine is a way of life not just a job, so Marines apply their disciplined approach to achieve goals in all aspects of life. This requires conscious attention to balancing work and personal growth.

Sometimes this decision is one of pure economics based on your Marine's needs and goals and whether they can provide financially for themselves and their family. A good tool, similar to the MOS Roadmap, is the "Lifecycle of the Military Consumer" resource sheet developed by the Department of Defense to map out the financial milestones in one's military career. Areas of interest are listed along with resources specific to each topic, such as keeping finances in order, financial challenges of moving, money management skills, and meeting financial challenges after leaving military service.

Continuation and Reenlistment

As your Marine approaches the end of their commitment, they will need to make a decision about continuing their journey with the Marine Corps. Officers may continue to serve as long as they meet promotion requirements for their rank. Enlisted Marines may choose to extend their contract or reenlist during the reenlistment window, generally six months to one year before their contract reaches completion.

Professional skills are required to remain eligible for service. Training—physical, mental, and professional—will be demanded and constantly assessed as your Marine progresses in rank and responsibility.

If an enlisted Marine is eligible to reenlist, they have shown proficiency in their MOS. Sometimes, if the Marine Corps has no room for a Marine within their MOS, but the Marine has a proven record of proficiency to advance, the Corps will offer them a lateral move to a similar or different MOS where there is room.

Officer advancement in the Corps is determined by selection boards of Marines who review the officer's records and compare them with those of their peers. The Marine's performance must show the potential to assume more responsibilities at a higher rank. It is an up or out process.

For those eligible to continue serving, the choice to stay or go is almost as dramatic as joining the Marine Corps.

Some Marines cannot see life any other way. One seasoned, unmarried, gunnery sergeant knows himself well and had this to say about continuing his life in the Corps:

> Re-enlistment? Hell yes. I'm fifteen years in, and if I get selected for warrant officer, I'm staying for thirty years. I got out of the Marine Corps once, and I remember exactly why I came back. This career gives me a great sense of purpose that I couldn't find anywhere else. It's my calling. And it's fun as hell. It's taken me throughout the four corners of the world, exposing me to wonders I never thought I'd see, and I've made friends throughout the globe.

The decision to stay in or leave the Corps may be something your Marine chooses to discuss with you. As my father often said, "My children may not want my advice, but I will always have an opinion in some matters." For me, when that day comes, it will be a decision our son and his wife have to make. I see my role as supporting their decision. Each family situation is unique. Family businesses, a parent's health factors, or other unique situations may impact this important decision. Have an honest conversation with your Marine, and respect that this is ultimately their choice.

Finding one's purpose and calling in the Marine Corps is a powerful reason to stay. And not many jobs offer the military's comprehensive benefits. Once a Marine adds new dynamics to their family, such as a spouse and children, the choice to continue in service affects everyone in the family. A Marine must consider all options.

One Marine reflected:

> Reenlisting again feels like a long time away
> since I just reenlisted, but I probably will not again.
> I want to do what is best for my family. I haven't
> been able to spend much time with them and care
> for them in the way I want to. It's going to be a big
> decision. When the time comes to make that choice,
> it will be a family discussion, and we will figure it out
> together.

While the Marine above feels it is time to get out due to his family circumstances, others are staying in for their families, as this Marine spouse described to me:

> We are now only a few years from retirement,
> and it is wild to think our whole family has dedicated
> twenty years to the Marine Corps by the time he
> retires. There have been moments of great joy, but
> also pain and sacrifice. To me, that is life, military or
> not. We deal with a multitude of hurdles nonmilitary
> families cannot comprehend; this has impacted our
> family by bringing us closer together.
>
> Of course, there have been struggles, the greatest
> being it's been hard to maintain my own career, but
> then I am thankful that his income allowed me to
> stay home with our children. And with the Internet,
> remote work or working from home is a great avenue
> for spouses. We have missed our extended family,
> yet we have seen six of the seven continents in this
> beautiful world. There is always a give and take.
> Our own little crew has faced five moves and five
> deployments, with more on the way. The challenges
> of this lifestyle have molded our family into a strong
> unit and strengthened our marriage.
>
> It has been one of the most incredible journeys,
> and I cannot imagine my life without this experience.

Every time my husband came up for reenlistment, we discussed it together. But our eye has always remained on the prize: retirement. We see the long-game and know that the benefits for us outweigh getting out. When we cross the finish line of military service, we leave with a steady retirement for life, health care, and college tuition for one of our children. We also had our children "free of charge" within a military hospital, we have no debt, and countless travel photos of us all across the globe. I am also confident we are leaving with the knowledge and capability to go after whatever is next.

This spouse went on to say that her family's time in service has been made more fulfilling because the entire family is engaged. They have decided that military life, while fraught with challenges, remains the best fit for them. Everyone in the family is working to do their part to make it to retirement.

In some cases, it is actually a Marine's spouse that encourages them to stay in, as this Marine acknowledged:

My wife supports me by understanding and pushing me in my achievements. Many times she's believed in me more than I did! I am finishing my time in the Marine Corps as a warrant officer. She has been extremely supportive over the years as I spent many months away on various TADs, (temporary additional duties). I worked as an interpreter for a joint agency for several years and was pretty much constantly on the road or back long enough to prepare for another trip. She even delivered our baby by herself while I was deployed to Korea. In short, she supports me by caring.

I reenlisted three times before I accepted appointment to warrant officer. I never intended to stay in past my original five-year enlistment.

I already had my bachelor's before I enlisted and received many job offers as a corporal. Yet I just couldn't get out. I've been very lucky in my career and have gotten some pretty amazing assignments and opportunities. My wife has played a huge hand in keeping me in, especially when orders to Hawaii were on the table!

Deciding unexpectedly to continue on in service is a common theme for Marines. Twenty years can feel like a very long time when Marines enter boot camp; however, as they draw closer to getting out, they are often struck by thoughtful reasons to stay. Surprising world events can impact career decisions too:

To be honest, my Marine did not intend to reenlist after his initial eight-year contract. We had been dating since before he went to boot camp, and finally married when he had completed six years as a Marine. He had already completed three deployments to Iraq by then. Our plan was for him to transition out around the time we had our first child. I had a solid earning potential and was working on my master's degree so that we could live on my income while he went back to school or trained for a job in law enforcement.

Unfortunately for us, his initial contract ended in 2008. At that time, the stock market was crashing, the economy was unstable, and many jobs were not hiring new positions. The local police departments all announced hiring freezes for at least a year. We couldn't afford to stay in the same area on just one income, but if we moved to a more affordable area, I would have a hard time finding a new job. So we made the decision together that it was best for him to remain in the military for the job stability and the benefits. We knew at the time that reenlisting

to the twelve-year mark probably meant a twenty-
year career. The most difficult challenge at the time
was accepting that we would probably never live
near family, so reenlisting meant that our children
would grow up far from grandparents and cousins.
We are now seventeen years into it and are happy
with the decision to remain in the military. Yes, we
have always been far from family, but he has had a
fulfilling career, is close to completing his degree, and
will enjoy tremendous pension and health benefits
when he retires in a few years.

Consider what motivates a Marine to choose to leave active
duty. The warrior culture of the military can take its toll on the
Marine and on the Marine's family. Or perhaps another job offer or
service opportunity may come along that better meets the needs of
the family, and it is time to depart from active-duty service. Everyone's journey is unique, in life and the Marine Corps. Staying in is
not best for everyone, so for those who choose not to reenlist, programs are available to help ease the transition back to civilian life.

A few Marines and their families shared their ultimate deciding factor when determining the best time to get out of active
duty. One Marine Corps family had a very positive journey with
their time in service; however, they found that having their child
changed their relationship with military life. The Marine enlisted
at a more advanced age than most of his peers, and they endured a
high operational tempo with deployments before their child. Once
the deployments showed no sign of slowing down, they decided
they no longer wanted to continue such rigorous separations anymore. The couple said:

We decided to start our family in our late
thirties. Now leaving a young infant behind in
order to serve a fourth deployment in six years
does not have the same allure as it did with the first
deployment! We feel blessed to have our child. It has

also made it all the harder to leave, as we want to support our family the best way we can. Ultimately, this change in our family dynamic solidified our decision not to reenlist. All the time away from family, either physically, emotionally, or both, wasn't in our best interest anymore.

This family is fortunate that the Marine's spouse was able to pursue a lucrative career during their time in service, which has provided a financial safety net for them. They also shared:

The best way our family has supported our Marine is by establishing a healthy level of independence. He has a spouse with a career. This aided our Marine because he knew his spouse was developing a social network that provided strength and support in addition to the Marine Corps family. A spouse with a career has also allowed our family to plan for a future that might not include a full military retirement and pension, which has alleviated stress for the Marine in making choices about his future.

Marines who are not eligible or who decide not to continue serving on active duty, will separate out of the Corps or possibly apply to serve in the Reserves.

Transition Planning

The Marine Corps pledges to "Make Marines, win battles, and return quality citizens to our American society." Marine mentors, career retention specialists, and the Career Transition Center are some of the resources available to transitioning Marines.

Your Marine's transition from military service to civilian life may impact you and your lifestyle directly or indirectly. Understanding the motivations, processes, and resources available helps you support your Marine when that time comes.

The timeline for transition can begin one year out from end of active service (EAS) for enlisted Marines or end of obligated service (EOS) for officers. For retiring Marines, the process can begin two years away from a projected retirement date. These are officially mandated start points, but all Marines should reflect on their personal, financial, and professional goals throughout their careers to better prepare. This might include:

- Assessing future needs—new lifestyle goals, skills, budget.

- Gaining knowledge, skills, and abilities to thrive.

- Identifying and nurturing support networks.

- Applying for schools, training, jobs, or service opportunities that are in line with interests, hobbies, and passions.

Transition Readiness Seminars

As your Marine makes their way out of service, they are required to attend a Transition Readiness Seminar (TRS). The DoD mandates that every Marine is offered a complete and comprehensive transition support package. In cooperation with Veterans Administration and Department of Labor representatives, this workshop for your Marine and their spouse is coordinated by the local base installation to provide transition readiness.

A Marine's unit career recruiter will provide advice on their career options, timelines, and pre-separation counseling. Steps in the transition process should begin at least one year prior to separation and two years prior to retirement. Your Marine should schedule their appointment with a pre-separation counselor and acquire these documents to create a package of information, an individualized transition plan.

The Corps and Veterans Administration recognize that the whole family serves, encouraging your Marine and their spouse to use the Transitional Assistance Program (TAP). TAP includes classes, workshops, and counseling to aid their transition to the civilian world. Marines will be educated on their VA benefits (home loans, education, healthcare) and resources that can help them meet career-readiness standards for separation from military life.

As part of a personal finance class for transitioning military members, your Marine will create a twelve-month budget. Additional resources will help them fine-tune their pathway choices and options for their next career step: further education, job search, or perhaps starting a business.

Transition Success Comes in Many Forms

The life of a transitioning Marine has many different paths. A reservist's career and life of service can occur either from the start after Marine boot camp or OCS, or after one's first obligation is met, or after twenty years of service. Reservists can continue to serve until retirement at age sixty-five, when they gain full retirement benefits.

As a private citizen following military retirement, one might consider serving the community through jobs supporting JROTC programs in high schools or NROTC programs in colleges. A Marine can enjoy volunteer opportunities as a Marine Corps League member too. Career growth and development can occur at many stages in a Marine's career, with and without the uniform. Being realistic about the "what ifs" and "what next" scenarios is a good attitude.

One Marine shared that he planned his transition right from the beginning of his service. Following his MOS Roadmap, he trained, deployed, stayed the course, and enjoyed career success. Throughout his journey, he also worked on a Plan B. He imagined what he wanted his life to look like thirty years from his start in the Marine Corps. He made choices and set goals from the beginning of his enlistment. Planning his life before, during, and after the Corps helped him look ahead toward multiple possibilities of achieving a pension.

His journey began before boot camp, with frequent visits to talk to veterans at the Marine Corps League about their choices in life. He heard the pros and cons of how to set one's path. A Marine officer told him that, if he had it to do over again, he may have enlisted first to learn more about the life of an enlisted Marine, then applied for other options to complete a degree using the GI Bill. Then becoming an officer, on active duty or in the Reserves, could have been a viable option. After hearing such reflections, this Marine chose to enlist, then as he approached the end of his first term of enlistment, he assessed his options and became a reservist.

Focusing on financial goals and personal development from the beginning of his career, this Marine set the course for success for the rest of his life. He says that sacrificing short-term pleasures to help him achieve long-term growth was a key point that contributed to his success. His Corps leaders had always advised and encouraged him to complete professional military education courses (PMEs), update his records of achievements, and take college courses.

Steps like these toward personal and professional development can prepare a Marine for successes beyond active duty and set them on a course that makes them a better Marine and, later, a better civilian.

Kim Johnson's journey from boot camp through transition is another great example. Her story began as a college dropout due to poor grades, and eventually led to a stellar twenty-year career in Marine aviation. She then chose to pursue the college degree she had denied herself twenty years earlier. She spent time in a community college to regain her academic confidence and skills, and set her sights on getting a degree from the University of Virginia's prestigious Frank Batten School of Leadership and Policy. Leadership qualities she learned from the Marine Corps compelled her to become a leading advocate for other veteran students. She established a chapter of the Student Veterans Association at the university and was recognized for her numerous contributions by the university president at her graduation ceremony.

As Kim found, a variety of support networks are there for those who choose to obtain a degree using the GI Bill benefits, including programs such as the Student Veterans Association and the Warrior Scholar Program.

Marine For Life (M4L)

The Marine Corps supports the Marine For Life Network—Marine reservists who serve as points of contact and resources for transitioning and retired Marines to reconnect to their civilian communities. Their ultimate goal is to connect Marines and family members to relevant resources that support their personal and professional goals after service. M4L representatives are passionate about assisting transitioning Marines and family members. The personal contact and developing a network of support has proven to be critical to Marine transition success. M4L reps are embedded in communities throughout the US, building and sustaining networks of Marine-friendly employers and local resources. Transition training and tools enable those who are planning to transition to educate themselves for future opportunities.

Parents can play an important role in this transition process. Connecting your Marine to a M4L representative, member of the Marine Corps League, or VFW in your local community could be the beginning of a meaningful relationship for the entire family.

The leadership and mentorship provided by M4L is also paramount. Whether giving advice on transition milestones, providing contacts for networking, or listening to stressors, the mentorship is genuine, concise, and greatly appreciated. The Marine For Life Network cannot promise a Marine or family member a job, but through their network of representatives, they can connect your Marine to valuable resources to support their transition!

Chapter Nine

Ceremonies and Celebrations

ONCE A MARINE, ALWAYS A MARINE, so *Once a Marine Parent, Always a Marine Parent*. And as a Marine parent and member of the Marine Corps family, you will benefit greatly from celebrating and supporting the special Marine Corps ceremonies and traditions with your Marine throughout their active duty career and long after your Marine transitions out of the military.

Marine Corps Birthday Ball

Just as our own birthday provides an opportunity to celebrate and recognize a year gone by, the Marine Corps birthday, November 10, marks an annual celebration of the entire Corps family. Avoid scheduling other big events on this day, as the Marine Corps birthday is an important and often emotional tradition. Many Marines continue to gather together or get in touch on the Marine Corps birthday long after their time in service.

Every Marine Corps unit hosts their own Marine Corps Birthday Ball to reflect on the current year's events and pay their respects through a grand event steeped in tradition.

Attending the Marine Corps Ball is an honor, filled with both celebration and ceremony. Proper etiquette is in good style, as well as acknowledging the important events of the evening. There will be a ceremony that lasts about an hour, including speeches, a cake-cutting ceremony, a birthday message from the current

Commandant of the Marine Corps (CMC), and the reading of
Gen. John A. Lejeune's birthday message (he was the 13th CMC).

One spouse reflects:

> This is my last year as a military spouse, and it's
> these formal occasions I'll miss most. As I look back
> at all these years, I think the Marine Corps Ball is
> how I have marked the passage of time. I started out
> as a new spouse with no idea about all this pomp and
> circumstance, and now I'm an old hand at it all.

Another spouse noted:

> Marine Corps Balls have been a great way to
> include our families in our lifestyle. For me, all the
> history, pomp, and circumstance make you proud to
> be part of the Marine Corps. We have been blessed
> to be able to take our parents, our kids, and other
> family and friends. They get to enjoy hearing a little
> about their Marine, and they get to support them and
> encourage them on this occasion. Plus, after you have
> enjoyed the ceremony, having your family present to
> celebrate what you do in life while eating, drinking,
> and being merry is a wonderful experience.

One Marine Corps family had two very different ball experiences during their time overseas on the Marine Security Group
program. They were stationed in Dubai, United Arab Emirates.
The spouse recalls:

> At the first ball in Dubai, my sister-in-law flew
> out from Indianapolis, Indiana. There has never
> been a person in my family to really leave the
> United States, and no other military affiliations on
> my husband's side of the family. My sister-in-law
> called my husband's dress blues an "outfit" instead
> of uniform and all sorts of fun things! She got to
> experience her first military ball. It was exciting to

do it right and be in Dubai! She had no idea about the ball or what it stood for until that night. She sat at the head table and listened and saw firsthand what the birthday ball was about. My husband and I both loved the gift of her presence and sharing the experience with her.

At the second ball we had the pleasure of my mom flying out to babysit our children. Everyone thought Dubai was just this beautiful and fun place— but what they didn't realize was how expensive it is. There are no such things as babysitters in Dubai, only full-time nannies. We were not interested nor could we afford such help. My mother flew out from Virginia just to watch our children so we could attend our last ball in Dubai together. She arrived the day before and managed to care for a two- and a three-year-old while suffering from jet lag!

Sometimes the best provision a grandparent or extended family member can provide for their Marine Corps family is to provide predictable and safe childcare for events like the ball. Another spouse said:

My in-laws planned their trip to see us around the Marine Corps Ball. My spouse had the additional responsibility of not just attending the ball but organizing the whole event! I really wanted to be there to support and encourage him and his fellow Marines in-country. With my in-laws in town, they watched our daughter, and we were both able to enjoy the evening knowing she was in the best hands possible.

Parents attending the ball with their Marine often feel a greater appreciation for the ceremonial traditions of the Corps as well as pride in their Marine's participation in this formal event. If you have the opportunity to attend a Marine Corps Ball, go!

Wetting-Down Party

If formality is not your style, perhaps you will have a chance to enjoy a wetting-down party, an informal social gathering to honor a promotion. A Marine who is promoted will lay down a copy of their promotion warrant on the bar during the party—sometimes until it is soaked through. The promoted Marine typically pays for the party's drinks, alcoholic or not, with half or all the pay difference from the old rank to the new rank. If several Marines are promoted simultaneously, they frequently have a larger party, celebrating all the promotions together. Volunteering as the designated driver would be a valuable gift for a wetting-down! If the newly-promoted prefers not to partake in an alcoholic wetdown, they can instead be thrown into a body of water. The actual promotion ceremony (before the wetdown) is far more formal and marks the beginning of a new chapter for the Marine.

Promotion Ceremony

Promotion in the Marine Corps is an exciting time, and it signifies two things: more responsibility and more pay! The ceremonies generally follow similar guidelines, whether the Marine is enlisted or an officer. The Marine may not be promoted prior to the effective date of their promotion. At the ceremony, the promotion warrant is read out loud by a presiding official, always senior to the Marine being promoted. The Marine will reaffirm the oath from the presiding official. Finally, the Marine's new rank insignia is pinned on by individuals of the promoted Marine's choosing.

While getting promoted is special enough, one of the best moments for families to share in is pinning the new rank insignia onto the Marine.

A spouse of an enlisted Marine remembers her husband's rank pinning at US Army Garrison (USAG) Yongsan, South Korea:

> I was beyond excited to pin on my husband's new
> rank at his promotion ceremony. It was the first one
> I had ever been to, even though he had served for six

years already. While he is the Marine of the family, we work as a team to get through this life together, and it meant a lot to me that I could participate in his special day. It coincidentally lined up with my in-laws' visit to Korea, and so he surprised his mother the day of promotion by asking her to pin rank as well. Our parents are beyond supportive but, often due to our location in the world, they cannot always be present for the other major Marine events in his life like Hail and Farewells or awards he's received. Sharing in the promotion ceremony together has been a memory we will treasure for years to come.

Another spouse recalls her Marine officer's promotion in Oahu, Hawaii:

A special time for our family was when my husband was promoted right after our first daughter was born. His parents made a special visit from out of state for a few weeks to see our new daughter and be part of his pinning ceremony. His parents took turns pinning him at his ceremony, which I know was very special for him. This was a very pivotal time in my husband's career. Having his parents' full support for what he does, even when it is scary and unknown, not only supports him but supports me as his wife. I have always been able to call their home my home when he is away. They try to be there for us when things are both good and hard, which has been the ultimate blessing.

If parents or extended family members cannot be present for the promotion ceremony, they can still be supportive by requesting photos, sending a card, or making a congratulatory phone call.

As one family's Marine was promoted to the rank of captain during a deployment, the spouse shared:

My five-month-old baby girl and I were visiting

my family. We made big signs and took pictures of them to congratulate him!

You can always find a way to share and spread a little extra joy.

Parades

Parades are a common Marine Corps custom, typically held to mark important events such as a Change of Command, promotion, retirement, or award presentation. They are different in nature than a hometown parade marching down a main street. Ceremonial in nature, they often involve guests of honor, other Marines, and family and friends.

Parades require much planning and practice by the Marines who march in formation. Often a band performs "The Marines' Hymn," and other parade-related music created by John Philip Sousa for the Marine Corps. Seeing Marines marching with precision and grace is inspiring.

One of the Corps' best regularly-scheduled parades is the Evening Parade at the Marine Corps Barracks, Washington, DC, held on Friday evenings during the summer. This parade is a universal symbol of the professionalism, discipline, and *esprit de corps* of the United States Marines. The ceremony reflects the story of Marines throughout the world. The performance of music and precision marching features "The President's Own" United States Marine Band, "The Commandant's Own" United States Marine Drum and Bugle Corps, and the Marine Corps Silent Drill Platoon.

Another notable Marine Corps parade is the Sunset Parade, held against the backdrop of the Marine Corps War Memorial in Arlington, Virginia. This parade also features the music of "The Commandant's Own" Drum and Bugle Corps and the Silent Drill Platoon. The Sunset Parade is open to the public at no charge, and reservations are not required. So if you find yourself in the Washington, DC, area, plan on attending the Sunset Parade or the Evening Parade. Or attend a parade in your local area—these bands and performers travel to various military installations. Check your local calendar of events for dates and times. For up-to-the-minute information on performances in the Washington, DC, area, check the Marine Corps' official website under the "Parades" section.

Award Ceremony

Award ceremonies are similar to promotion ceremonies. Awards are given to the Marine by a Marine of higher rank or a guest of honor. A commissioned officer must preside over the ceremony, usually the highest-ranking official present, such as the company commander for a company formation or battalion commander for a battalion formation. The Marine is called to the front of the formation, the citation is read, and the Marine is presented the award. If family members are present, they are supportive bystanders and may take photos if cleared beforehand.

Award ceremonies, promotions, re-enlistments, and various other celebrations do not always wait for the Marine to be back home on US soil. Marines are serving all over the world, for varying lengths of time, and this can mean they receive their accolades in foreign countries—even on deployments. If a Marine's family is unable to be present, some commands make a special attempt to still include them. One family shared this story:

> One time, while my husband was deployed, I received a handwritten letter in the mail from his commanding officer. The letter talked about a medal my husband had just earned. It continued to say he was sorry we were unable to be there when my husband was awarded the medal. He ended it by thanking my sons and me for our continued support and sacrifice for our country. I called home to tell my family about it, however through their responses it was clear they didn't fully understand the significance of the medal or the letter. I feel like even though our family is happy for us, they don't truly understand the significance of the promotions and ceremonies. Over the last seventeen years, we have learned the value of our wider-spread military family.

They are the ones that completely understand and are there for the majority of our life events.

This spouse's story is a reminder of the importance of taking phone calls, and working to listen, respond, and be aware and informed of the journey your Marine is on. As involved as family members often try to be in planning for military life, Marine life is still highly unpredictable. A family shared with me:

> In Twentynine Palms, we were often notified only a few days before a promotion or a Change of Command ceremony. When our Marine took command or got promoted, there wasn't enough time for family to take part in the ceremony in person. However, they still made a point to call and recognize his achievement, which we appreciated.

As a Marine progresses through the ranks, letters of congratulations can be a valued gift. They tell your Marine that your heart is filled with pride, gratitude, and love for the hard work and sacrifice it took to accomplish worthy goals. An unexpected box of cookies, dry socks, or pictures of loved ones and the special events they missed are always nice, but be sure to include that you are proud of them for the sacrifice that comes with their service as well.

Change of Command

The Marine Corps Association describes the Change of Command as a "formal tradition, symbolizing the continuity of the authority of command. It is a transfer of total responsibility, authority, and accountability from one officer to another and is usually conducted before the assembled company of the command."

A Change of Command is a formal and reverent affair with a high attendance of personnel. The outgoing commanding officer and his relief usually proceed to the ceremonial area together, and the ceremony routine will generally include an honor guard to parade, singing or playing the national anthem, as well as an invocation and benediction.

Even with an event like a Change of Command, the simplest gift of being present might be the most meaningful for your family. One Marine spouse shares:

> My husband and I do not really receive gifts from our family members when it comes to his achievements in the Marine Corps. But the best "gift" by far has been our parents' physical presence at important events. His Change of Command ceremony has been one of our most memorable events! We were able to celebrate and enjoy everyone's company. His brother came in from out of town, and two extremely close friends that are like our family members flew in for the event. We were surrounded by so many people of both past and present that have impacted our lives. Some of these people were people who had only been present for a small portion of our journey, yet they came.
>
> I believe their presence was just as impactful to our lives as those we have known for years. Words cannot describe how blessed we felt to have these people take time out to come. I believe we learned a new life lesson that day: if you can be present in someone's life for an occasion to celebrate, go! You may think it does not matter, but it does matter! Your presence brings the gift of remembrance of a great chapter together, a sense of love to the other person's soul. You might represent and give the perfect embrace of someone who could not be at the event. Your hug/handshake/smile is the gift needed for this one moment.
>
> We will never forget that day and how loved we felt by seeing all those faces. Since then, we try to pass that amazing feeling forward and attend all the events we can for others.

Post and Relief

The Post and Relief ceremony is different from a Change of Command because it is a ceremonial assumption of a particular duty. Marines and their family members are generally invited to attend a Post and Relief ceremony to observe the "passing of the torch" to greater duty responsibilities and position. The former official will give a speech, speaking to the merits of the new leader. A speech is given by the new official, recognizing a duty well done. There may be a ceremonial passing of responsibility through a material item, such as a noncommissioned officer sword.

Hail and Farewell

A Hail and Farewell can be held at multiple levels but leans toward being a more personal affair. The celebration recognizes the new Marines and bids farewell to those leaving. A gift may be presented to the more-senior Marines as they leave, honoring those with billets of more significant responsibility. On the Marine Security Group tours, the unit is generally much smaller. Marines present one another with a special cultural item that is symbolic of their location. The family involvement at a Hail and Farewell is to be present, attentive, and supportive.

One spouse stated:

> As we were overseas, I recorded my spouse's Hail and Farewell for family and friends. We were protective of our fellow serving Marines and did not post it online. However, I shared it with my family when we saw them in person. At the farewell, all the Marines said something notable about my husband's leadership. It was a great delight for our parents to listen to the accolades the Marines had for him. I also greatly appreciated that my husband and his fellow Marines acknowledged the support my daughter and I had given them during the tour.

Dining In/Dining Out

Dining In, also known as mess night, is a formal dinner with ceremony reserved for members of a specific company or unit.

Similar ceremonial traditions take place at a Dining Out, but spouses and guests may be invited.

A Marine spouse recalls a Dining Out ceremony in Germany:

> Our unit made a thoroughly enjoyable evening for us all. Not only did they help to organize childcare on site at the hotel, but they also allowed the spouses to attend! I had never been to a formal Dining Out event, I only knew when my spouse attended a mess night or Dining In, he always came back really excited and fueled with energy. It always sounded like a great night full of laughter and camaraderie. To finally experience it as a spouse, I will always remember that night. One of the best moments was when the guest of honor presented water from the Belleau Wood fountain, everyone was able to drink the water from the sacred site. Belleau Wood is where the Marines earned their nickname of "devil dogs" during World War I. I have attended many balls, ceremonies, and promotions over the years, but the Dining Out is one of my most favorite and treasured memories I have with my Marine.

Family Days

Family Days in the Marine Corps represent a variety of reasons to come together, from seasonal events to goodbye gatherings and reunions. Family Days have also garnered the loving nickname "Mando-Fun" (mandatory fun) from the celebrations of the unit or battalion. The digital age makes it more important than ever to get families out of their homes and together for some real in-person face time. Most of the time, the Marine will not have a choice in attendance; they must come and represent themselves at the function, and may be expected to bring their spouse and children. Parents and other extended family members of Marines are welcomed and encouraged to join their Marine for the day as long as they have been invited by their Marine and have permission to be admitted to the location where the Family Day is taking place. This day is an informal way to meet everyone your Marine works with on a daily basis.

Organizers of the event, such as the unit readiness officer and other volunteers, have usually worked long and hard to organize all aspects of the day, providing a venue for Marines and families to meet and get to know one another, solidify the bonds of the unit, and build cohesion. To attend is respectful, and one might find that, even when mandatory to attend, it becomes real fun, as this Marine family found:

> We all have the tendency to roll our eyes at
> mandatory "Mando-Fun." I know I used to. However,
> especially after I became a new mom and we were
> thousands of miles from family due to our duty
> station in Hawaii, I started really looking forward
> to Family Days. Our FRO (family readiness officer)
> at the time always shared great ideas at these events
> and sparked plans for other events that got the
> spouses out of their homes in a particularly heavy
> deployment season. We went on hikes, we had simple
> coffees, and we learned and remembered that more
> than one of us was missing our spouse. One holiday
> party was particularly memorable: Santa drove by
> on a fire truck, there were bouncy houses, a karaoke
> contest, and a big, wonderful meal. Again, we were
> all grumbling because for some reason that's what
> we thought we needed to do … but what a folly!
> We had a great time. Everyone is going through the
> same thing at one time or another in the military
> community. Family events remind you that you are

not alone. I now encourage families to come out to Family Days. Meet your fellow battalion members. You might just have fun and find a new friend.

Send-offs to and Returns from Deployment

Deployments are a busy, emotional time for those deploying and their loved ones sending them off or welcoming them home. Departures and homecomings may include large gatherings or just a few individuals, take place on an installation or at a transportation checkpoint, and be planned far in advance or within hours of notification. Each situation is unique and depends on the location and type of deployment and the role of your Marine in the deployment. Please handle with care and consider what your Marine and other family members need most from you to support them during such high-emotion days.

One spouse shares:

> Every goodbye and every welcome home is slightly different. Depending on if we have family there, before we had kids, or how old our kids are. We have been blessed to have family who love us and respect my husband's choice to serve his country and my choice to follow him wherever it may take him. I am extremely close to my family but one thing my parents realize is that my place is with my husband. The priority has been keeping our family unit whole.
>
> Sometimes at welcome homes it has been just me (spouse), and other times we have had family from all over in attendance. When we do have family at the welcome homes, they have respected the fact that our kids might need some extra Dad time, and he may need to kiss his wife a little longer! When they have attended, they do not stay all night. They share a meal with us and then leave our family to ourselves for at least the first day. Since I have been a mom, I

now realize how that may be hard for the mom of the returning service member. That knowledge has made me love and respect my mother-in-law even more.

We also know who we are, and we have come up with the best way for us to say our goodbyes. My husband is a loving, dependable, and honorable man, but when it is time to say goodbye, he is ready to go, so we have agreed that short and sweet is the best for us personally. He needs to get his head on the mission, and I need to keep the family running. It is hard for him to see us hurting and vice versa. We hang out 'til the bus gets there, we give kisses and hugs, he gets on the bus, and then we leave. No hanging out. Sometimes we cry a little but that is okay, it is part of loving someone. But this method gives my children a clean break. They can start to process what is going on instead of waiting to watch the bus leave. All families and all people are different, so it is important to know your Marine and yourself. I am lucky enough that we process similarly, but if you are not you can come up with a compromise where you each get enough of what you need to make it the least difficult process it can be.

Another family noted that they have never been close enough in location to have family attend a homecoming event, but they did schedule the spouse's parents to be in attendance for the Marine's goodbye.

We had just had a new baby, and I was very worried about carrying the load by myself while he was gone. It mentally and emotionally boosted me to have my parents at my side as we bid our Marine goodbye for his deployment. We knew it would be better to not have anyone around for the coming home. We needed peace, time, and quiet to readjust as our own little family first. Then we were able to schedule some leave time and go visit everyone.

Whether your Marine is single or has a family, let them set the tone for what they need for send-offs, homecomings, and simpler events like Family Days. Ask them what role they would like you to play. Then consider your own needs as well. If you decide to offer in-person support, keep in mind that the nature of military orders may mean last-minute changes of plans. Try to keep your travel plans flexible. If you decide you do not want to travel to your Marine, that is okay too. Just as your Marine has the option to invite you, you can say yes or no to do what's best for you. What you may be able to do one time may not be possible the next. Set expectations and boundaries that create a positive situation for everyone.

Your Marine may decide to come to you. Before the visit, have a thoughtful discussion about the scope of celebrations you both have in mind and what your Marine is most looking forward to experiencing. For example, big family gatherings may be part of your traditions. Your Marine may not always want big events. Sometimes having free, unscheduled time is exactly what they want when they come home. The daily life and routine of a Marine is packed with required meetings, training classes, work, and physical exercise. Offering your Marine a chance to "do nothing," go nowhere past the front gate of your home, and enjoy a quiet backyard retreat may be just what they need and want most. In their unpredictable lifestyle, having the comfort of home, a few friends, and peace and quiet will make for a memorable visit.

Memorial Services

Families provide support in joyous moments and sad times as well. When the death of a loved one occurs, people gather to honor, remember, and pay their respects to families of the deceased. The Marine Corps is no different. A memorial service is a solemn occasion to remember the life or lives of those who have died. It may be held by a specific unit to honor their fallen. It may take place on a specific day to commemorate lives lost in combat or in service to their country. D-Day, 9/11, the landing at Iwo Jima, Memorial Day, or the Beirut bombing of 1983 are significant moments that Marines pause to remember. A formal presentation is made, and a wreath-laying ceremony is conducted, following specific protocols.

In the event of a death on active duty, a funeral or burial service is conducted according to the wishes of the deceased Marine or their next of kin. It may be conducted following military protocols or in a less formal setting. These occasions can be held in a religious house of worship, a cemetery, a field, or even a bar. The place does not matter, nor does the script for the ceremony. This is a time to gather, celebrate the lives lost, and recommit and honor the sacrifices of the Marines and families.

Transition Recognition

Marines are released from active duty for a variety of reasons. Regardless of the time in service, a transition ritual is recommended as a sincere gesture of appreciation for the Marine's time in service. The Marine Corps may not formally recognize someone who is completing their contract obligation in a ceremony. Family and friends can host a party, offer to set up a dinner at a restaurant, and let everyone pay their own way. A backyard barbeque is perfect if it offers a time to celebrate this Marine's service. The stress and anxiety that come when a Marine faces the uncertainty of the future can be assuaged for the time being when they are reassured that they are appreciated. This occasion gives the Marine a chance to thank the guests for their support and friendship, before, during, and after the Corps.

Retirement Ceremony

When the time comes to celebrate and recognize a Marine's retirement from a long career of faithful and honorable service, the Marine Corps hosts a retirement ceremony. Retirement ceremonies are filled with excitement, emotion, and exhaustion. With the Marine's assistance, the command develops an invitation list with names and addresses of fellow service members, family, and friends the Marine would like to be in attendance. The date and location is determined in advance to ensure that all essential members of the event can be present. Awards, letters of appreciation, and other gifts are thoughtfully prepared in advance. The ceremony is often followed by a reception or meal paid for by the Marine.

With many ways to honor a retiring service member, it is best to ask the retiring Marine what they prefer. Some enjoy a simple, small, private ceremony of immediate family and friends and a quiet after-party. Others want to include all the bells and whistles. Overall, the theme should be in honor of one long chapter ending and the excitement of a new beginning.

Amid the formalities of the ceremony, your Marine will bid farewell. Preparing this speech is a necessary part of closure for your Marine, causing them to reflect on their past, their mentors and peers, the Marines they led or served with, some who died too soon, and their family members, who sacrificed much to support them for those many, many years. This reflective process helps prepare them for this significant transition.

Leaving the Marine Corps, for any reason, is filled with mixed emotions. Part of the process includes similar logistics for a non-retirement transition. While celebrating their accomplishments, your Marine is also stepping into the answers to questions they and their family have been asking themselves about where to live, and whether this transition begins with a new job, more education, travel, family needs, or other personal desires. By American standards, a person leaving the Marine Corps at the twenty- or thirty-year mark may be considered too young to retire from work. A spouse's career, proximity to extended family, and many other factors are considered in these decisions. Your Marine is thinking about this future, which may already be in motion, while also dealing with the emotions of moving on from a known lifestyle.

Any family members and guests who can attend a retirement ceremony are in for a very special experience: part history lesson, recollection of the years of service, and part display of patriotism to honor the Marine's dedication and commitment. The gathering is with those who want to celebrate this person and to cheer them on to the next chapter in their life. What a happy and exciting time! So much love and laughter, tears and tall tales, friends and fond memories.

As a Marine spouse, I had a special prayer that carried me through thirty-nine and a half years of my husband's service: "God grant that my Marine will return home after every exercise, every deployment, and every conflict that puts him in harm's way. And I pray that he will have a loving and supportive family to return home to." On the day of his retirement, God answered my prayer. My husband retired, but as long as our son still serves, my prayer continues for him and his family!

Etiquette

If you are able to attend a Marine Corps event in person, take time to understand its significance and your role, the proper attire, and any special protocols. Most Marine Corps celebrations and ceremonies are formal events that require at least business casual clothing. Ask your Marine to help you select what to wear (or not wear). The Marine Corps is a conservative and traditional service, and you want to spend your time at events enjoying the ceremony, not worrying about your clothing or what may be expected of you.

Learn more about the event's typical agenda, including when food may be served. Pay attention to etiquette for invitation responses, arrivals and departures, greeting Marines and guests, and the timing and formality of speaking or clapping. If you are asked to participate in the ceremony, understand and practice your role.

Be aware of what is considered appropriate conduct for a guest, and make your Marine as proud of you as you are of them!

Gifts

Attending ceremonies and celebrations in person is the most special gift. With great distances between family members, parents and grandparents arriving in person for big events is a treat for all.

That might mean costly airfare, as well as the need to be fit and able to travel. If you can, it is a beautiful gift to give your time and presence, but many other options exist, as this story from a Marine Corps spouse shows:

> Our family has always been our biggest supporters. They can't actually attend promotions, homecomings, or changes of command, so they work to support our Marine in other ways, like wearing his unit's swag and putting the sticker on the cars they drive. My niece added our Marine to the hero wall at her school during his deployment as part of her school's celebration of veterans. They sent his favorite chips (that can only be bought in Pennsylvania) by the case when he deployed, as a small thank you for all he does during the year.
>
> These may seem like little things, but they mean a tremendous amount to us all. Support can happen in many different ways, and they do not need to be large gifts to mean something. A simple thank you from the heart carries the most meaning for us.

Small gestures of support can feel big to the supported. Purchase a Marine Corps T-shirt, and wear it proudly. Gather members of your community to pack care packages for Marines. Participate in local veterans projects. Your work on the homefront reminds others who don't have service members in their families that sacrifices are still happening every day.

This Marine's parents were only able to attend some of his big achievements in person, but they continued to support him throughout his day-to-day life as a Marine:

> My family has supported me during my time in the Marine Corps by video chatting with me during holidays so I can be a part of the holiday with the

family even when I am gone. They have also sent me
care packages or flown out to see me in person no
matter if I was stateside or overseas. My family has
always been a huge supporter of me and my military
career no matter what. Especially when I chose to go
overseas for the next three years! They have had my
back 100 percent of the time. Both my parents keep
me up to date with everything that's going on back
home and send me pictures. They sometimes post on
social media an achievement I have accomplished,
saying how proud of me that they are or just telling
me they love and miss me.

Even with miles between them, families can remain present in
the ongoing excitement, trials, ceremonies, and celebrations of a
Marine's career. Gathering photo albums or video compilations of
the Marine's career from various family members and friends can
make for a keepsake all will enjoy for years to come.

While most families are happy and satisfied with the gift of
in-person presence or the gift of childcare during events, some
also still love to give or receive physical gifts. The Marine Shop and
the Marine Corps Museum gift shop in Quantico, Virginia, have
several curated mementos for retirement and other special occasions. Personalized items are also available from Marine-friendly
online shops. Consider your Marine's personality and special moments in their Marine Corps career to guide you toward the most
meaningful gifts.

Closing

Staying Faithful

THE JOURNEY YOU TRAVEL WITH YOUR MARINE starts by taking the first step and keeping the faith through the rest. I have shared this philosophy with my own children as they entered into the new role of a parent. A parent's journey can be measured in stages of endurance:

Physical endurance: Birth to about age five. Can I keep up with the late-night feedings, dirty clothes and dishes, get enough sleep, finish a meal, outrun a toddler when they are determined to escape, or just maintain their energetic pace?

Mental endurance: Ages six to fifteen. Can I out-think them? Can I raise them with the right words when they ask the hard questions, or explain how my acts of discipline like rules and boundaries are for their own good? Can I find the right opportunities to share values and set the right examples?

Emotional endurance: Age sixteen to the end of their life, or yours. Can I live with the decisions they make that I have no control over? How can I process all these emotions when they spread their wings of independence and learn how to fly (or drive)?

This endurance is tested even further as Marine parents and grandparents. We have even more reasons to worry and care. So how do we endure? How do we keep the faith?

Have faith that your Marine is well trained and well led. They pledged an oath to live by an elite code of behavior every day, on and off duty. They have chosen to serve and to sacrifice their freedoms for the sake of the freedoms and liberties of others.

Keep faith in the Marine Corps to "Make Marines, win battles, and return quality citizens to our American Society."

Have faith in yourself that you have what it takes to be a Marine parent. Your hopes, best wishes, thoughts, and prayers go with your Marine, and they know it.

I have witnessed firsthand the support of parents and families, from the first days of recruitment through deployments, transitions, retirement ceremonies, and beyond. Across America, support is especially evident with those caring for their wounded, ill, or injured, or praying at the headstone of their Marine's grave. Your support is meaningful and appreciated.

Find faith in something bigger than yourself. In the darkest times, when all I could hold onto was my faith, I found the serenity prayer to be most meaningful:

> "God, grant me the serenity to accept the things
> I cannot change, courage to change the things I can,
> and wisdom to know the difference."

When my children were younger and finding their way, I offered this prayer to them:

> "Go with God leading you, the angels
> surrounding you, and may you come home safely
> with great stories to tell."

Though the days of parenting seem long, the years pass quickly, so enjoy the journey. The pride and memories will last forever.

Semper Parents. Semper Family. Semper Fidelis!

Marine Corps 101

THIS INFORMATION IS COMMON KNOWLEDGE for most Marines as a result of study and practical experience. I share it here to give you a broader understanding of the Corps. You can find this and more on the official Marine Corps website, Marines.mil.

Role and Mission of the Marine Corps

Marines deploy around the world for reasons varying from wartime operations to natural disaster support. US Code, Title 10, Subtitle C, Part I, Chapter 507, Section 5063 states:

- The Marine Corps shall be organized, trained, and equipped to provide fleet Marine forces of combined arms, together with supporting air components, for service with the fleet in the seizure or defense of advanced naval bases and for the conduct of such land operations as may be essential to the prosecution of a naval campaign.

- The Marine Corps shall develop, in coordination with the Army and the Air Force, those phases of amphibious operations that pertain to the tactics, technique, and equipment used by landing forces.

In 2018, General Robert B. Neller, USMC, 37th Commandant of the Marine Corps testified before Congress: "As the nation's crisis response force and force in readiness, Marines remain forward deployed, ready to fight and win tonight. As Marines have always done, we will continue to seek new opportunities and develop solutions that maintain an overwhelming tactical advantage over any adversary."

Ronald Reagan, fortieth US president, noted the importance of the Marine Corps: "Freedom is never more than one generation away from extinction. We did not pass it to our children in the bloodstream. It must be fought for, protected, and handed on for them to do the same, or one day, we will spend our sunset years telling our children and grandchildren's children what it was once like in the United States when men were free." He also honored their service directly by saying, "Some people spend an entire lifetime wondering if they made a difference in the world. The Marines don't have that problem."

How the Marine Corps Is Organized

Three active-duty Marine divisions plus a reserve division make up the Marine Corps. The Marine Corps' leader, the commandant, reports directly to the Secretary of the Navy.

Each element and department of the Corps has a specific structure, determined by its size, location, and function. Some include a headquarters element at command levels, starting at the battalion and squadron levels, and at special commands at major bases, stations, and installations.

Infantry and Logistics includes a core of Marine units starting at fireteam level and gaining in size to form a squad, platoon, company or battery, battalion, regiment, and up to an infantry division or logistics group.

Aviation includes squadrons of flying and non-flying units with up to two dozen aircraft. Their crews and departments are about the size equivalent of a battalion. Groups are formed with three or more squadrons, equivalent to a regiment. Wings are formed from three groups, equivalent to a division.

Marine Expeditionary Units (MEUs) are forward presence, crisis response units that are normally forward-deployed on a consistent rotation. They are capable of conducting conventional and select maritime special purpose missions.

Marine Expeditionary Brigades (MEBs) are able to respond to a full range of crises and contingencies and can serve as enablers for joint/combined forces.

There are three Marine Expeditionary Forces (MEFs), and each is normally formed with a headquarters element, ground combat element, aviation combat element, and logistics combat element. MEFs are deployed during major conflicts, to decisively defeat the enemy and to preserve and protect the national interests and democratic values held by the US and its allies.

Marine Forces Reserves (MARFORRES) may be located anywhere in the US. Many Reserve units have readiness officers to assist with communication, readiness, and deployment support.

Command elements work together to get the job done, combining forces to include Ground Combat Element, an Aviation Combat Element, and a Logistics Combat Element, to form a Marine Air-Ground Task Force (MAGTF). MAGTFs work together, in scalable combined arms teams.

Marine Corps Core Values

No two Marines bring the exact same values to the Corps. Each comes into the Marine Corps having been shaped over time by family, religion, and culture. The Marine Corps spends great physical and emotional capital to help recruits become Marines. "Marine" is not a title given; it is an honor earned.

The transformation from young person into Marine starts with those values, recognizing the potential in each recruit or candidate to become the best version of themselves. It shapes and influences new beliefs, skills sets, and behaviors, including the core values.

The Marine Corps understands the need for, and benefits of, instilling a common set of values among all Marines. It has been proven that teams are significantly more successful when they share a common vision and adhere to common values. Strong Marines who believe in the same ideals, adhere to the same code of behavior and ethics, and work to accomplish the same mission are an unbeatable force. These core values form the cornerstone of a Marine's character, the guiding beliefs and principles that give strength, influence attitudes, regulate behavior, and bond Marines into a force that can meet any challenge.

Honor

Honor is the foundation of a Marine's character, the quality that empowers Marines to exemplify the ultimate in ethical and moral behavior: to never lie, cheat, or steal; to abide by an uncompromising code of integrity; to respect human dignity; and to have respect and concern for each other. It represents the maturity, dedication, trust, and dependability that commit Marines to act responsibly, be accountable for their actions, fulfill their obligations, and hold others accountable for their actions.

Courage

The heart of core values, courage is the mental, moral, and physical strength ingrained in Marines that sees them through the challenges of combat and the mastery of fear. It inspires them to do what is right, adhere to a higher standard of personal conduct, lead by example, and make tough decisions under stress and pressure. Courage is the inner strength that enables a Marine to take that extra step.

Commitment

Commitment is the spirit of determination and dedication within members of a force of arms that leads to professionalism and mastery of the art of war. It promotes the highest order of discipline for unit and self and is the ingredient that instills dedication to Corps and country. Pride, concern for others, and an unrelenting determination drive Marines to achieve a standard of excellence in every endeavor. Commitment is the value that establishes the Marine as the warrior and citizen others strive to emulate.

The Marines' *Esprit de Corps*

Esprit de Corps is the ethos, the characteristic spirit that describes the behavior, drive, and qualities of excellence of Marines.

- Every Marine is a rifleman, a crucible of tough training, and of physical and moral courage. Marines are ethical warriors—steeped in core values, service, and sacrifice. Small-unit leaders are biased for action, trusted, accountable; will accomplish any mission; and have love for their fellow Marines.

- Marines exhibit institutional ethos: An expeditionary mindset—willingness to "live hard"; a war-fighting philosophy over war-fighting methodology; a young force, frequently deployed, always challenged.

Principles Marines Live By

- Marines are focused on combat; ready, relevant, and forward deployed; innovative, adaptable, and versatile. Marines do what is right for the nation, keep their honor clean, and take care of their own.

- The Marine Corps is a naval expeditionary force; an integrated combined arms organization of complementary air, ground, and logistics components; and a good steward of the nation's resources.

Marine Corps Oath

In the Marine Corps, enlisted personnel and officers must take an oath to affirm their commitment to defending the Constitution and, by extension, the Corps. The oath is sworn by every enlistee before enlistment and by every officer candidate before commissioning. Marines take the oaths again as they reenlist or are promoted. The military oath is a combination of constitutional requirement, historical influence, and centuries-old custom. The oath of office for officers is the same oath sworn by all individuals elected or appointed to an office of honor or profit in the civil service, except the President. A Marine's oath is a commitment to God, country, and Corps.

Enlisted Personnel Oath

"I, [your name], do solemnly swear (or affirm) that I will support and defend the Constitution of the United States against all enemies foreign and domestic; that I will bear true faith and allegiance to the same; and that I will obey the orders of the President of the United States and the orders of the officers appointed over me, according to regulations and the Uniform Code of Military Justice. So help me God."

Officer Oath

"I, [your name], do solemnly swear (or affirm) that I will support and defend the Constitution of the United States against all enemies foreign and domestic; that I will bear true faith and allegiance to the same; that I take this obligation freely and without any mental reservation or purpose of evasion; and that I will well and faithfully discharge the duties of the office on which I am about to enter. So help me God."

Traditions

Marine Corps traditions and customs are what set the Corps apart from the other services, an ongoing source of pride that firmly connects the past and present, a constant reminder of the glory and valor of Marines who have come before, and a beacon for new Marines to follow. Traditions bind members of the Corps together.

Some of the traditions, lingo, and heritage of the present-day Corps hail from naval origins. Many years being shipboard left their mark on the Corps and you catch glimpses of naval heritage in the Corps' traditions, symbols, and customs. More importantly, examples of the core values can be seen in action and in how they are woven throughout the culture of the Corps.

"Semper Fi," the Marine Corps Motto

Semper Fidelis, or *Semper Fi*, as it is used in the Marine Corps, is Latin for "always faithful," underscoring the core value of commitment and demonstrated by a Marine's loyalty and fidelity to other Marines. Marines are always there for one another and show unwavering loyalty to God, country, and Corps. A powerful example of *Semper Fi* on the battlefield is the Marines' pledge to never leave another Marine behind.

"The Marines' Hymn"

Playing of "The Marines' Hymn" is a deeply revered Marine tradition, a tribute to warriors and a reverent account of the proud battle history of the Corps. The hymn's verses tell of the honor and glory Marines earned in battles on every conceivable foreign shore, and exemplifies the singular mission and passion of the Corps.

The oldest of the service songs, "The Marines' Hymn" has no record of its author. The melody was written by Jacques Offenbach and performed for the first time in 1859. The words first appeared in 1898 on a recruiting poster.

When "The Marines' Hymn" is performed outdoors, Marines stop and come to attention. If performed indoors, they stand and come to attention. Civilians do not have to stand and come to attention but, out of respect, should stop talking and wait for the hymn to finish.

By custom, "The Marines' Hymn" is the last piece of music played at all ceremonies where a band is present. This includes changes of command, the Marine Corps Birthday Ball ceremony, parades, and other appropriate ceremonies.

"The Marines' Hymn"

From the Halls of Montezuma
To the shores of Tripoli;
We fight our country's battles
In air, on land, and sea;
First to fight for right and freedom
And to keep our honor clean;
We are proud to claim the title
Of the United States Marines.

Our flag's unfurled to every breeze
From dawn to setting sun;
We have fought in every clime and place
Where we could take a gun;
In the snow of far-off Northern lands
And in sunny tropic scenes;
You will find us always on the job—
The United States Marines.
Our flag's unfurled to every breeze
Here's health to you and to our Corps
Which we are proud to serve;
In many strife we've fought for life
And never lost our nerve;
If the Army and the Navy
Ever look on Heaven's scenes;
They will find the streets guarded
By the United States Marines.

Marine Corps Birthday—November 10

For many years prior to 1921, the Marine Corps did not seem to celebrate its birthday with any ceremonies, pageants, or parties. The closest it had to an official birthday was July 11, 1798, when President John Adams signed a bill officially establishing the Corps as a permanent military force under the jurisdiction of the Department of the Navy. However, in 1921 Major General John Archer Lejeune issued a Marine Corps Order summarizing the history, mission, and tradition of the Corps, and directed that it be read annually to every command on November 10 as a way to honor the birth of the Marine Corps. This became known as General Lejeune's birthday message.

Thanks to General Lejeune, the Marine Corps birthday is celebrated on November 10—a very important date for all Marines that is often celebrated with prescribed activities. The affairs can be small and take place in remote locations, or they can be grand and transform into a birthday ball. Larger celebrations are often in garrison and showcase troop formations, call for Marines to be in period dress, or incorporate parades when practical. The birthday ball celebrations are formal events with Marines in their dress uniforms and spouses in formal evening attire for a ceremony and dancing. Each command determines the manner in which the birthday is celebrated.

Whether big or small, certain events generally always take place. General Lejeune's birthday message is always read. A social gathering often includes a special meal. The cake-cutting ceremony is a crowd favorite. The first piece of cake is presented to the oldest Marine present; the second piece to the youngest Marine present. When the age of the youngest Marine is made apparent, it highlights the youth and vitality of the Corps.

The Marine Corps birthday is a time for all Marines, uniformed and veterans alike, to honor Marines who have served and fought in every clime and place, and celebrate today's Marines who carry on the tradition. Attend the celebration and see firsthand the pride and love of the Corps.

Symbols and Icons

Marine Corps Emblem

The Eagle, Globe, and Anchor make up the official emblem of the Corps. Marines are fighters from the sea, supported by and supporting naval operations.

- The Eagle represents an American force in readiness.

- The Globe represents the training, mentoring, advising, fighting, and deploying around the world.

- The Anchor signifies their relationship with the Department of the Navy and their values of honor, courage, and commitment.

Ceremonial Swords

The Marine Corps NCO sword, adopted in 1859, is only carried by non-commissioned officers (NCOs) and staff NCOs and is used only for ceremonial purposes. Prior to 1859, the USMC officer's sword, called the Mameluke, was in use. From 1825 to the present, all Marine officers possess a Mameluke sword.

Marine Corps War Memorial

The Marine Corps War Memorial, also known as the Iwo Jima Memorial, located in Arlington, Virginia, is a symbol of this grateful nation's esteem for the honored dead of the US Marine Corps. The statue depicts one of the most famous events of World War II (the flag raising at Iwo Jima) and the memorial is dedicated to all Marines who have given their lives in defense of the United States since 1775.

The thirty-two-feet-high memorial figures are shown erecting a sixty-foot bronze flagpole from which a cloth flag flies twenty-four hours a day. The granite base of the memorial has the names and dates of every principal Marine Corps engagement since the founding of the Corps burnished in gold, and the inscription: "In honor and in memory of the men of the United States Marine Corps who have given their lives to their country since November 10, 1775." Also inscribed on the base front is the tribute of Fleet Admiral Chester W. Nimitz to the fighting men on Iwo Jima: "Uncommon Valor was a Common Virtue."

Customs and Courtesies

Military courtesy is the traditional form of politeness of arms. Military courtesy is a form of discipline that must be accorded to all ranks on all occasions—toward senior officers and juniors to show appreciation, respect, and support for them as fellow Marines. Military courtesy stems from and contributes to the Marines *esprit de corps*. Soldierly courtesy and discipline are twin virtues.

United States Flag

Just as the Eagle, Globe, and Anchor represents the Marine Corps, the United States flag represents the nation. The US flag is often displayed alongside the Marine Corps flag. When the US flag is passing in a parade or review, those out of uniform remove their headgear, turn toward the flag and stand at attention and, when the flag is six paces in front, place their right hands over their hearts until the flag passes. Placing their right hands over their hearts is also done when the flag is being raised or lowered. Similarly, those present in uniform render the military salute and cover their hearts during the National Anthem when the flag is displayed and during the Pledge of Allegiance.

The Salute

The salute is a military courtesy, gesture of respect, and sign of comradeship among military service personnel. The salute is a greeting between an officer and an enlisted member, or between a junior officer and a senior officer. For all services, the salute begins with the junior rendering the salute and the senior returning the salute. The appropriate civilian greeting is to simply say, "Good morning, Ma'am" or "Good evening, Sir."

In the past, armed service members raised their weapons, or shifted them to the left hand, and raised their right hand to signal friendly intentions. This hand salute gesture is a traditional greeting used by the military of all nations.

Types of military salutes include the hand salute, the rifle salute at order arms, a rifle salute at right shoulder, and another rifle salute at present arms. "Eyes Right" is another type of military salute that is rendered by troops in rank when passing in review.

Cultural Characteristics

Uniforms

Marine Corps uniforms serve functional, traditional, and distinctive purposes that set Marines apart from others and provide protection and increased operability. Historically, uniforms have been the product of a Marine's wartime environment.

Uniforms vary by rank and are divided according to their purpose: field uniforms, dress uniforms, and service uniforms. Field uniforms are camouflaged combat utility uniforms designed to suit every climate and place and to adapt to the mission. Camouflage patterns for woodlands and desert are digitally generated with the Marine emblem integrated into the pattern. Service uniforms are normally worn when reporting for duty or to parades, ceremonies, social occasions, and other official functions. The formal evening dress blue uniform is most typically associated with the Marine Corps.

Medals and ribbons signify accomplishments (unit, personal, and professional). The colored cloth represents the various campaigns, battles, or regions in which the Marines served, and are also represented in battle streamers affixed to the top of the Marine Corps flag. If a specific unit participated in a campaign, the unit flag bears that battle streamer. Insignia on the uniform identify special qualifications or training.

Rank

Rank is the immediately identifiable sign of achievement displayed on every uniform. Rank signifies individual responsibility and accountability for personnel, equipment, and mission.

Enlisted Rank

The enlisted structure has nine separate ranks, or steps, divided into three subgroups. The junior-most group (40 percent of enlisted active-duty) consists of privates, privates first class, and lance corporals. Marines who attain the next ranks of corporal and sergeant (35 percent of enlisted personnel) earn the distinction of becoming noncommissioned officers (NCOs). The most senior enlisted ranks are the staff noncommissioned officers (SNCOs), ranging from staff sergeant to sergeant major.

More than other services, the Marine Corps allows a greater level of leadership at the NCO level. NCOs are the corporals and sergeants responsible for the lives of their soldiers in combat. They carry with them the unbroken traditions of duty and dedication to their assigned mission.

NCOs and SNCOs are successful in all facets of leadership, especially in combat operations. NCOs, for example, head patrols and manage high-dollar-value equipment. They are able to make quick, appropriate decisions on the battlefield. Technology is such that a patrol with global-positioning-system equipment is able to call for targeted airstrikes on an enemy location. The NCO leadership allows a high level of operational control by the Marines with "boots on the ground."

Warrant Officer and Officer Rank

Warrant officers provide leadership and skills in specialized fields. Warrant officer ranks range from warrant officer 1 (WO1) to chief warrant officer 5 (WO5). They are a small group (11 percent of officers) who started as enlisted personnel but who later completed the Warrant Officer Basic Course. This course provides all WO1s with a common officer training experience regardless of the technical occupational field for which they were selected.

Officers begin their journey as company grade officers (57 percent of the active-duty officers), starting with second lieutenant, then first lieutenant, then captain. The ranks of major up to colonel are field grade officers (32 percent of the officer structure). Senior leaders of the Corps are the general officers (fewer than 1 percent of the total officer population).

The primary function of commissioned officers is to provide overall management and leadership within their area of responsibility. Commissioned officers do not specialize as much as enlisted members and warrant officers, with certain exceptions such as pilots or lawyers.

Pay Grades

The Marine Corps ranks (enlisted, warrant, and officer) are not the same as their pay grades. Pay grades are administrative classifications used to standardize compensation across the military services. The "E" in E-1 stands for "enlisted" while the "1" indicates the pay grade for that position. The other pay categories are "W" for warrant officers and "O" for commissioned officers. Some enlisted pay grades have two ranks. For example, at the E-8 level, the Marine Corps has two career paths at the same pay grade; whether a Marine is a master sergeant or a first sergeant depends on that person's job. The same is true at the E-9 level. Marine Corps master gunnery sergeants and sergeants major receive the same pay but have different responsibilities. E-8s and E-9s have fifteen to thirty years on the job and are commanders' senior advisors for enlisted matters. The sergeant major of the Marine Corps is an E-9 and is the spokesperson for the enlisted force at the highest levels of the services.

Military Time and Date

Military time is based on a twenty-four-hour clock, which can be confusing to those accustomed to the twelve-hour a.m./ twelve-hour p.m. time standard. The twenty-four-hour clock is the military standard and the preferred time assignment for hospitals, emergency personnel, and the shipping and navigation industries.

Consider operational matters like training exercises, deployments, ship movements, and aircraft flights: the military must often coordinate with bases and personnel located around the world in other time zones. To make sure everyone is synchronized to the same time zone, the military sets all operational clocks to Greenwich Mean Time (GMT), Greenwich, England. The military refers to this time zone as "Zulu Time" and attaches the "Z" suffix for clarity.

For most daily activities, Marines use the local twenty-four-hour clock as a reference. So when asked to be at work by 0700, that means work starts at 7:00 a.m., local time. "The commander wants to see you at 1500 hours" means being in the commander's office by 3:00 p.m., local time. (Most Marines I know would be there fifteen minutes early!) Marines are expected to know and use military time in their workplace.

The preferred method of recording dates is as follows: 18 Jan 22 (numeric day, first three letters of the month, and last two numbers of the year).

Military = Civilian	Military = Civilian
0001 = 12:01 a.m.	1230 = 12:30 p.m.
0100 = 1:00 a.m.	1300 = 1:00 p.m.
0200 = 2:00 a.m.	1400 = 2:00 p.m.
0300 = 3:00 a.m.	1500 = 3:00 p.m.
0400 = 4:00 a.m.	1600 = 4:00 p.m.
0500 = 5:00 a.m.	1700 = 5:00 p.m.
0600 = 6:00 a.m.	1800 = 6:00 p.m.
0700 = 7:00 a.m.	1900 = 7:00 p.m.
0800 = 8:00 a.m.	2000 = 8:00 p.m.
0900 = 9:00 a.m.	2100 = 9:00 p.m.
1000 = 10:00 a.m.	2200 = 10:00 p.m.
1100 = 11:00 a.m.	2300 = 11:00 p.m.
1200 = noon	2400 = 12 midnight

Jargon

Welcome to one of the trickiest but most fun parts of joining military life—learning a new language, Marine jargon! Military culture has its own ways of dressing, acting, and talking. The talk can seem like code and can be hard to pick up at first. Much of the jargon stems from Marine and naval history, and acronyms are used widely. There are many more terms and acronyms than listed here, but these will get you started.

Common USMC Terms

All hands	All members of a command
As you were	Resume former activity
Brig	A place of confinement; a prison
Carry on	The order to resume previous activity
Chit	A receipt or authorization, a piece of paper
Field Day	Barracks office or general cleanup
Hatch	A door or doorway

Head	Latrine or toilet
Oorah	Motivational shout uttered by Marines
Roger	Affirmation of a question or statement
Secure	Stop, finish, end, make fast, put away in storage
Square away	Straighten, make shipshape, or get settled; inform or admonish someone in an abrupt manner

Common USMC Acronyms and Abbreviations

ALMAR	all Marine message
BAH	basic allowance for housing
BAS	basic allowance for subsistence
BEQ	bachelor enlisted quarters
BLT	battalion landing team
BN	battalion
BOQ	bachelor officer quarters
BQ	billeting
CACO	casualty assistance calls officer
CAX	combined arms exercise
CG	commanding general
CNO	chief of Naval Operations
CO	commanding officer
COLA	cost of living allowance
CONUS	continental United States
CWO	chief warrant officer

DEERS	Defense Enrollment Eligibility Reporting System
DI	drill instructor
DIV	division
DoD	Department of Defense
DoDEA	Department of Defense Education Activity (base schools)
DPAC	Division Personnel Administrative Center
DSN	Defense Switching Network (military phone system)
DVA	Department of Veterans Affairs
EAS	end of active service
EOS	expiration of obligated service
EFMP	Exceptional Family Member Program
ETA	estimated time of arrival
ETD	estimated time of departure
FMF	Fleet Marine Force ("The Fleet")
G-1	group/regiment/division manpower (admin)
G-2	group/regiment/division intelligence
G-3	group/regiment/division operations
G-4	group/regiment/division logistics
G-5	group/regiment/division plans
G-6	group/regiment/division communications electronics
GPAC	Group Personnel Administration Center

GSA	General Services Administration
HM**	refers to helicopter squadron (e.g., HMM-264)
HQMC	headquarters, Marine Corps
IG	inspector general
I&I	inspector & instructor (reserve unit staff)
I&L	installation & logistics
IMA (or IA)	individual mobilization augmentee
IPAC	Installation Personnel Administration Center
IRR	individual ready reserve
JAG	judge advocate general
JRC	Joint Reception Center
LDO	limited duty officer
LES	leave and earnings statement
LZ	landing zone
M4L	Marine For Life Network
MACG	Marine Air Control Group
MACS	Marine Air Control Squadron
MAG	Marine Aircraft Group
MAGTF	Marine Air/Ground Task Force
MALS	Marine Aviation Logistics Squadron
MARFOR	Marine Forces
MARFORCOM	Marine Forces Command
MARS	military affiliated radio station

MARSOC	Marine Special Operations Command
MASS	Marine Air Support Squadron
MAW	Marine Aircraft Wing
MCAS	Marine Corps Air Station
MCB	Marine Corps Base
MCCDC	Marine Corps Combat Development Command
MCCS	Marine Corps Community Services
MCI	Marine Corps Installation
MCLB	Marine Corps Logistics Base
MCO	Marine Corps Order
MCR	Marine Corps Reserve
MCRC	Marine Corps Recruiting Command
MCRD	Marine Corps Recruit Depot
MCT	Marine Combat Training
MCTFS	Marine Corps Total Force System
MCX	Marine Corps Exchange
MEB	Marine Expeditionary Brigade
MEF	Marine Expeditionary Force
MEU	Marine Expeditionary Unit
MEU(SOC)	Marine Expeditionary Unit (Special Operations Capable)
MFR	Marine Forces Reserve
MLG	Marine Logistics Group

MOA	memorandum of agreement
MOC	military occupational code
MORDT	Mobilization Operational Readiness Deployment Test
MOS	military occupational specialty
MP	military police
MREs	meals, ready-to-eat
MSB	mobilization support battalion
MSC	major subordinate command
MSSG	MEU service support group
MTACS	Marine Tactical Air Command Squadron
MWCS	Marine Wing Communications Squadron
MWSG	Marine Wing Support Group
MWSS	Marine Wing Support Squadron
NAF	nonappropriated funds
NCIS	Naval Criminal Investigative Service
NCO	noncommissioned officer
NCOIC	noncommissioned officer in charge
OSD	Office of the Secretary of Defense
OCONUS	outside the continental United States
OCS	Officer Candidate School
OIC	officer in charge
OIT	on installation trainer

OOD	officer of the day
OPS	operations
OPSEC	operational security
PCS	permanent change of station
PDS	permanent duty station
PFT	physical fitness test
PME	professional military education
POA	power of attorney
POC	point of contact
POV	privately owned vehicle
PP&O	plans, policies & operations
PSC	Personal Services Center
PT	physical training
PTAD	permissive temporary additional duty
PX	post exchange
QOL	quality of life
RAP	Relocation Assistance Program
RC	reserve component
RED	record of emergency data
REGT	regiment
RLT	regimental landing team
RPG	rocket-propelled grenade
RTC	reserve training center

S-1	squadron/battalion manpower (administration)
S-2	squadron/battalion intelligence
S-3	squadron/battalion operations
S-4	squadron/battalion logistics
S-6	squadron/battalion communications electronics
SACC	substance abuse counseling center
SAPR	sexual assault prevention and response
SAR	search and rescue
SARC	sexual assault response coordinator
SATO	Scheduled Airlines Traffic Office
SDO	staff (or squadron) duty officer
SECDEF	Secretary of Defense
SECNAV	Secretary of the Navy
SGLI	Servicemembers Group Life Insurance
SJA	staff judge advocate
SMP	Single Marine Program
SNCO	staff noncommissioned officer
SQD	squadron
SSN	Social Security Number
TAD	temporary additional duty
TAP	Transition Assistance Program
TAPS	Tragedy Assistance Program for Survivors
TBD	to be determined

TBS	The Basic School
TECOM	Training and Education Command
TLA	temporary lodging allowance
TLF	temporary lodging facility
TMO	Traffic Management Office
TOS	time on station
TR	transportation request or transfer
UA	unauthorized absence
UPFRP	Unit, Personal, and Family Readiness Program
VA	Veterans Affairs
VM**	refers to fixed-wing squadron (e.g., VMGR-252)
WestPac	Western Pacific
WO	warrant officer
WTI	weapons and tactics instructor
XO	executive officer

Acknowledgments

MANY PEOPLE made the stories and information in this book come to life. First, I extend my thanks to my family. My parents, Vincent and Pauline Sottile, and my parents-in-law, Fred and Avis Regner, all in heaven now, set the finest examples of love and support to us as parents and as grandparents to our children throughout our many years of service in the Marine Corps. My children, J. and Katie, Julia and John, have been supportive of this book project for the duration, allowing us to dedicate this time away from them and their young families. To my Marine son, Mike, his wife Erin, and their children, thank you for allowing us to share your journey. Our relationships have grown and changed with each passing year. From your courtship, wedding, the birth of your children, many moves, and deployments, I have enjoyed this privilege and learned firsthand what it is like to be the parent and grandparent of a Marine family for more than twenty years. To my husband, our journey as a team began many, many years ago. My support for your career journey was rewarded with your support for this book. Your knowledge and technical expertise, feedback, and network of great individuals led me in the right direction to write something of which we can both be proud.

Thank you to the publisher and team at Elva Resa for taking a chance on me as a first-time author. You had faith in me to write about the topics and stories in this book that reflect a realistic look at the lifestyle, support, and information parents and extended families would want to know or need to know about in a relevant and responsible way.

Lindsay Swaboda, without your contributions and editing talent, I would still be typing. We shared the journey in such a special way. I will always be your biggest fan and will enjoy reading your positive spirit through your blog, *Uplifting Anchor*. Keep writing, my friend!

My sincere thanks to General Robert Neller, the 37th Commandant of the Marine Corps, who told me, "First, go talk to Sergeant Major Green," and to Sgt. Maj. Ronald Green, 18th Sergeant Major of the Marine Corps, whose constant personal interest held me accountable to produce something of true value. I hope you are as proud of your Marines and their families, and the stories they shared, as I am. I will forever be in the debt of the Marine Corps leadership for allowing me the privilege to interview the best of the best: Marines, chaplains, drill instructors, recruiters, Wounded Warriors, and many more. This includes the Manpower and Marine Corps Community Services (MCCS) leadership, Mr. Jeff Bearer, Ms. Marie Balocki, and Sgt. Major Sean Isaacson, for introducing us to the civilian department heads known respectfully as civilian Marines at Quantico, Virginia, and many others throughout the Corps. They enabled me to get the facts of policies, programs, and procedures for family readiness, behavioral health, transition readiness, and the Wounded Warrior Regiment. Thanks go to Maj. Gen. Austin "Sparky" Renforth, former commanding general of the Marine Corps Recruit Depot (MCRD), Parris Island Command, for the opportunity to get a behind-the-scenes tour from Capt. Adam Flores and to interview drill instructors and MCCS Director Deanna Simpson and her staff. Thanks go to Maj. Gen. James "Chip" Bierman and the great recruiting staff, Maj. Luke Sauber, and the staff noncommissioned officers (SNCOs) of Recruiting Station (RS) Frederick—your insight was eye-opening to the role recruiters play in our Corps, all day, every day. A special appreciation goes to Annette Amerman, branch head and historian at the Historical Reference Branch, Marine Corps History Division, for writing an updated version of a Brief History of the Corps, including a generous look at the diversity of those who have worn the uniform.

Next, my gratitude and appreciation go to those parents who shared their personal stories, from recruitment through transition and beyond, as caregivers for the more gravely wounded, ill, and injured, and in the years of grief following the death of their Marines. To Mrs. Carla Hogan, the Gold Star mother of Cpl. Donald Hogan, Silver Star recipient: your goodness toward others, and your strength and courage to go beyond your grief, will always be a testament to the love you had for your son and his brothers-in-arms. Robin Carpenter is another example of the daily support she and her husband Jim have given to their son Kyle during the most difficult of days. You both are my heroes. Thank you for sharing, because it is often not in the nature of Marine moms to talk about personal sorrows. Mary Alice Monroe, you inspired me as a writer, telling me to think from the heart of a mom and the words would come. I have reflected on many scenes in your book, *A Lowcountry Christmas*, to imagine the "what if" and "what next" with faithfulness and prayer.

To a long list of Marine Corps SMEs (subject matter experts) who listened to my concepts in the early stages, helped me see what was being offered to parents of Marines and where the gaps might be, and agreed to be interviewed, offered advice, suggested a person to talk to, or helped keep me on track. You have been my go-to folks for guidance and support. This list is extensive, and I apologize for any unintended omissions. They include Col. Mike Shupp, USMC (Ret), who initiated the conversation with me about writing this book; Evonne Carawan; Bonnie Burns; Debbie Paxton; Chaplain Captain Larry Greenslit, USN, retired, and his spouse, Amy Greenslit; the Marines and spouses of The Basic School; Master Gunnery Sergeant Pat McLane Hackbarth, USMC, retired; Charlie Grow and Bob Sullivan at the Museum of the Marine Corps; Kim Bradley; Edward Nevgloski, PhD, Historian for the Marine Corps; Melissa Cohen; and Ann Todd, PhD.

My gratitude goes out to parents, Dr. and Mrs. Andrew Rogers, Mike and Joanne Whelan, and Michele Jewell as well as Sam Meek, Erik Tjornhom, and Kim Johnson whose passion was inspiring; and special friends, Antigone Doucette, Carol Lavoy, Erin Walerko, Cindy Fox, and Kelly Rupp, who kept cheering me on from the sidelines. Thanks everyone!

There are many nonprofit organizations whose leadership and friendships have allowed me to offer valuable information and resources to support this book. My thanks go to Wendy Lethin and Karen Gunther, Semper Fi Fund; Dave Coker and Brian Gawne, Fisher House Foundation; Bonnie Carroll, Tragedy Assistance Program for Survivors (TAPS); Jennifer Carazo, Sugar Bear Foundation; the Travis Manion Foundation; everyone at the National Military Family Association; United Through Reading; the USO; the Marine Corps League and Auxiliary; and the Women Marines Association. They all serve the needs of thousands and have dedicated their lives to supporting our Marines and their families. Their journeys began long before this book project, and I pray they continue to serve for many years to come.

www.ingramcontent.com/pod-product-compliance
Lightning Source LLC
Chambersburg PA
CBHW031301090426
42742CB00007B/550